# The Dream,
# the Movie,
# the Play

### by
### Grace Fiore

Foreword by Sal Rachele

Dear Ferris
"Happy Birthday"
May your year be filled
with joy —
Hope you enjoy my book —
if people could understand
my work they
would see an
alternate
perspective on
the human
experience
"It would give
peace a chance"
xo
Mom

# The Dream, the Movie, the Play

Published by: Grace Fiore
6517 W. 6<sup>th</sup> Street, Los Angeles, CA 90048, USA

First Edition: March 2017

Printed in the United States of America

ISBN: 978-0-692-84649-0

# Table of Contents

# Table of Contents

# Acknowledgements

*I would like to express my gratitude to all the classical and new age teachers who have contributed to my understanding:*

*Robert Adams, Ramana Maharshi, Nisargadatta Maharaj, Jesus, Adnan Sarhan, Jim Dreaver, Michael Jeffreys, Juan Pablo Giaradi, Edward Muzika, Eckhart Tolle, Deepak Chopra, Byron Katie, Buddha, Spinoza, Stephen Hawking, Jim Braden, Wayne Liquorman, Papaji, Darshan Singh, Ramesh Balsakar, Krishnamurti, Mark Twain, Tony Parsons, Democritus, Swami Vivekananda, Sri Ramakrishna, Aldous Huxley, Socrates, Shakespeare, Bhagwan Shree Rajneesh (Osho), Krishna, Les Visible, and my own inner teacher – the Infinite Source.*

*I would also like to thank my dear friend Sal Rachele, who has been a source of great inspiration and encouragement to me.*

# Preface

In discussing the essence or understanding of our existence on this planet, Einstein says, *"The human mind, no matter how highly trained, cannot grasp the universe. We are in the position of a little child, entering a huge library whose walls are covered to the ceiling with books in many different tongues. The child knows that someone must have written those books. It does not know whom or how. It does not understand the languages in which they are written. The child sees a definite plan in the arrangement of the books, a mysterious order, which it does not comprehend, but only dimly suspects. That, it seems to me, is the attitude of the human mind, even the greatest and most cultured, toward the mystery of God. We see a universe marvelously arranged, obeying certain laws, but we understand the laws only dimly. Our limited mind cannot grasp the mysterious force that sways the constellations."*

Einstein's message embraces recent discoveries of quantum physicists, neuroscientists and biologists.

Most scientists agree that we only use five to ten percent of our brain capacity. If we want to understand the intricacies and mysteries of life, we must learn how to use more of our innate abilities. Typically, those who have awakened more of this capacity seem to have done so through some sort of "grace" or through a lifetime of diligent study.

If we look at our present lives, we might wonder about the nature of our existence. Why are we here? Why do we endure sorrow and ultimately what we call death? The average life scenario lasts, perhaps, seventy or eighty years...and then this identity we are so attached to exists no longer. Religions have explained this as a passage to another stage of existence – such as heaven or hell. The theories are many.

In all humility, I wish to share with you what I have discovered in my studies of the great religions of the world, as well as the writings of the noteworthy sages and eminent scientists and philosophers. I will be including the theories of Einstein, Democritus, and the non-dual and New Age theorists that have contributed to my understanding. These are just a limited reflection of the ultimate truth. I present my thesis for your examination, hoping my presentation will enliven, enrich and ultimately bring a sense of joy and peace to your life.

The viewpoints in this book may require a vast change of perspective, and involve the ultimate giving up of identification with our conditioned and programmed perceptions of life.

I will examine how and why the identity we assume in our daily lives is total fiction, and give insight as to why this is so. Furthermore, I will introduce the theories that support this point of view. I invite you to go with me on this exciting journey through and beyond the dream world.
  --*Grace Fiore*

# Foreword

## by Sal Rachele

When Grace approached me and asked if I would write the Foreword, without giving it much thought I said, "Of course."

The subject matter herein is dear to my heart because it explores the core of the primary problem facing our world today – the belief in separation from the whole and the resulting identification with the ego.

This work offers solutions for a general audience – not just scientists, philosophers and spiritual seekers, but everyday folks from all walks of life.

This is no idealistic, instant enlightenment manual. Whether you are a seasoned explorer of the unknown, or just beginning to realize that there is a lot more to life than the 9 to 5, getting married, raising children, and such, the author (and the many contributors) are quick to point out that the path to enlightenment is not only the most rewarding path in life, but is often one of the most difficult.

We live on what I call, "the amnesia planet." This is because even when we know what is best for us, we tend to "forget" repeatedly. We have within us the knowledge of how to escape the pitfalls and traps of this world, but we often ignore this knowledge. The real question is, "How do we access this immeasurable knowledge and apply it in our daily lives?"

Unless you have been living under a rock, you have undoubtedly seen the vast rows upon rows of books on self-help, psychology, New Age, philosophy and related subjects that adorn your neighborhood bookstore. While some of these books may not be helpful, the answers are there for any serious seeker.

Although some might think the subject of this book is a secret, this knowledge has been freely available for millennia for those who are willing to look. Yet, we tend to reject anything that takes us outside our comfort zone. We have become creatures of habit, even though we know that most of our habits are destructive or, at the very least, extremely limiting. For most of us, life on Earth is like driving an eight-cylinder automobile on only two cylinders. We might eventually get to our destination, but the path will be long and arduous.

Why is this? The Buddhists would say it is due to our resistance, our attachment to the known, the comfortable, and the safe. This is a false kind of "safety" and is actually very dangerous. It is like a frog bathing in a pool of warm stagnant water at the edge of a river, with a long, hot dry spell approaching. If the frog doesn't jump into the moving water, it will shrivel up and die as the hot sun dries up the pool.

Someone once remarked, "The only thing constant in this world is change." If that is so, then embracing change should be on the top of our priority list of ways to cope with the problems of this world. It is imperative, if humanity is to survive, that we make significant changes.

This book goes far beyond self-help. It is not here to teach you how to make changes to your personality, lifestyle, income, or even beliefs. The purpose of this book is to assist you in going completely beyond the human experience.

What lies beyond? Very simply, it is the difference between waking and dreaming, between being the director and producer of your movie or play, and simply being one of the actors playing out your script.

This world is full of sleepwalkers, going through endless repetition and rote behavior, like hamsters on a wheel. Why do you think they call it the "rat race?" Isn't it time for something new? This is not another theory, belief, concept or idea, but something radically new, something revolutionary. Whether or not you acknowledge it, by picking up this book you are opening a door into a new way of living. You are making a declaration of intent to seek out the truth, no matter how uncomfortable or challenging it might be. I invite you to join the author in taking the ultimate trip, from fantasy to reality.

--Sal Rachele

*"No one can fail who seeks to reach the truth."*
--A Course in Miracles

The Dream, the Movie, the Play

# Introduction

## The State of the World

While it's undeniable that humans are capable of great love, we also have an unspeakable history of brutality, murder and war. Recorded history has shown that human beings have consistently oppressed those who are weaker than themselves or more vulnerable to attack. In examining the last 2,000 years, we see a series of atrocities: The Dark Ages, the Inquisition, "holy" wars, the Crusades, burning of witches, genocide of entire civilizations (such as the American Indians) and the discrimination of ethnic and minority groups. One look at the planet today shows major evidence of man's inhumanity to man.

It seems to some that we must endure and keep on marching, through irreversible time, in a world portrayed as wholly indifferent to our well-being, toward an inevitable ending of decrepitude and death.

Despite all our marvelous accomplishments, humans have been the most ferocious and destructive force on Earth—and the eternal question is, "Why?"

*"Sorrow is homemade, and, so far as the universe is concerned, unnecessary."*
—Aldous Huxley, Island

## The Alternative

There is a way to resolve the darkness that has driven our planet to the enormous problems we witness in the world today. A lack of awareness of the true nature of reality prevents the understanding necessary for acceptance of others, and the peace, goodwill and manifestation of so-called miracles.

The ability to comprehend the true nature of things is unrecognizable to most of humanity. The vision that the author describes herein can be reached through a complete re-education, including the relinquishment of outdated beliefs, attitudes and conditioning.

As a result of the scientific studies referenced in this book, it becomes clear that the world is not as it seems. It also becomes clear that benevolent forces are present in our universe. We can recognize and access these forces when we are open to looking at the nature of reality in a different way.

Socrates famously said, "The unexamined life is not worth living." Carl Jung was forever saying, "Wholeness for humans depends on their ability to own their own shadow." (This shadow is sometimes referred to as the "phantom self" or ego.)

Can there be a reconciliation and rehabilitation of our species from a competitive, aggressive, materialistic society, one in which many are depressed and find no joy in their lives, to an experience full of peace and benevolence? Must our species live in a deeply troubled condition…a psychotic existence? Or can we rise above our seeming circumstances?

It is the author's intention to negate the belief in the need for deep suffering that the average person on this planet experiences. This book seeks to prove that such suffering is avoidable.

You might ask, "How is it avoidable?" The author's reply is, "By understanding our true identity and the laws that govern experience on planet earth."

We must truly let go of everything we have been taught or conditioned to believe; the totality of what we thought we knew.

There is an alternative to a life of endless struggle and strife. Wise teachers throughout the ages have been giving us the answer. Now, in modern times, even science can show us the way out of endless conflict. In Chapter 3 of this book, there are numerous examples from different branches of physics that demonstrate the ideas being given herein.

In all of recorded history, there are numerous references to a supreme being or deity that supposedly controls everything from on high. Such an entity has been molded according to the beliefs and superstitions of each given age. Most religions offer a strict set of rules and commandments in order to appease such a capricious entity. Those who behave a certain way are promised salvation and a trip to the heavenly realms – essentially, escape from mortal life on earth. Of course, this whimsical god also offers severe punishment for breach of the rules and commandments, threatening sinners with a future of purgatory or hell.

There has been a perception of separation between the so-called "heavenly realms" and the "earthly kingdoms." The more enlightened among us have outgrown this dualistic system of heaven and hell and have determined that these are simply states of consciousness rather than actual places.

Yet, this book seeks to go beyond even this interpretation, to the idea that who we are is beyond all duality whatsoever. In other words, we are neither good nor bad, right nor wrong, light nor dark.

The Divinity we will speak of here refers to the absolute reality that exists beyond the realms of duality. To say that God is good is to misunderstand the nature of the Divine. The God we are speaking of is also known as the Great Mystery – beyond all concepts, ideas, conclusions, assumptions, beliefs and dogma. There can be no comparison, no judgment whatsoever if we wish to have a direct experience of the Divine. In the following pages, we will illustrate how to attain a state of Divine consciousness, or rather, how to remember a state of being that has always existed within us but is only recognized by a few.

Not surprisingly, those in the past who had a direct spiritual experience that goes beyond traditional religion have often been persecuted, ridiculed or simply ignored. A few have been worshipped and their teachings twisted and distorted.

True spirituality must include the idea that there is One Being, and that One Being includes everything that is, in all levels and dimensions. We seek to show, through various concepts, that every one of us is an integral part of that One Being, which we call the Divine.

To be truly free, you must come to understand that you are a Divine Being and remove your aspiration for the world to fulfill you. This unveiling of the higher vibratory frequencies available to us comes when we give up our idea of a personal self. Everything – all concepts, ideas and beliefs of the individual "I" have to go.

There is only one entity, called the Universal Self, or field of intelligence, that encompasses everything. All forms appear as projections of this Self. You are the fullness and majesty of this Universal Self. Human intelligence is a hindrance. Look at the world this lower level of intelligence has created. When we demonstrate the truth of who we really are (a manifestation of Divine Being), we will experience the freedom and joy that comes with this transformation of consciousness.

## Changing our Perspective

So why does the world appear so negative and violent? Where does this sense of struggle come from? Why is this drama such a tragic one?

It has been mentioned that the problem initially arises through our misunderstanding of who we are. By believing we are small, weak, isolated individuals living in a largely hostile universe, subjected to all manner of danger, needing to struggle to survive against outside elements, we devise elaborate systems of defense in order to protect what we believe is ours. We identify with our physical bodies and believe they are frail and helpless against the ravages of time.

How do these beliefs come about? At the age of two or three, when conditioning begins to solidify in the mind, the toddler identifies his own character; the baby is educated in the earthly dramas and roles he will play. Thus begins the formation of the phantom self, or ego. This sense of a separate self is the primary cause of suffering.

Many religions equate this sense of separation with Original Sin. While the Biblical story is largely allegorical (the apple, the tree, the snake, etc., are largely symbolic), the original problem is the belief in separation from God.

What happens to the child is that a mental construct is set up. The child is given a name, identity, gender and expectations of what he will experience in life. This is the persona – the character being played in the drama of life. This personality becomes the ego and its conditioning impacts us the rest of our lives.

The ego represents our shadow self, bombarding our existence with about 50,000 thoughts per day. Many of these thoughts are fear-based or negative due to the ego's identification with the mortal form.

True reality is covered up by our false programming. However, we often experience a sense of disillusionment that motivates us to find a deeper meaning to life. Without really knowing what it is that we are looking for, we may begin our journey of self-exploration. We then soon discover that awakening to our True Self involves more than just studying the works of enlightened teachers. We must unlearn most of what we have been taught. We must disassemble the false self.

For most of us, our sense of self involves an individual inhabiting a body – a human being. This is who we think we are. This is the "I" and the "me." To be free you must recognize that the imaginary character you personify is not who you really are. We have a Divine Self. This Self is our true nature. We do not need to search outside our Self. We are the Divine, but imagine that we are characters in this dream world. The imaginary self (the sense of being an individual) is at the root of every trouble we face. It is like a veil that separates us from true reality. It makes us a stranger in our own world.

You are not a human being animated by the Divine; you are the Divine experiencing itself as a human being. This book seeks to prove that statement.

## The Persona Does Not Really Exist

Mark Twain explains the nature of the personal "I":

*"You are not you. You have no body, no blood, no bones, you are but a thought. I myself have no existence; I am but a dream – Your dream. A creature of your imagination."*

Mark Twain also says:

*"Life itself is only a vision, a dream. Nothing exists; all is a dream. God-man-world-sun-moon. All a dream, all a dream; they have no existence. Nothing exists save empty space."*

It is a great relief when you become free of the personal "I" or "me." At that point you will find your identity not in story, experience or beliefs, but in Being itself; in the beauty, harmony and fullness of existence. You will still have a role in the story of your life and a character to play in the worldly drama – as a business or professional person, as an artist or musician, or as a mother or father. But you will know beyond a shadow of doubt that who you really are is more than this.

There will no longer be this deep-rooted belief system, based on the illusion that all objects in our surroundings are separate from us or outside us. We will no longer identify with the body's senses or conscious mind that creates a separate world of "me" and "you." The notion of being a personal entity separate from all other entities will lose its meaning.

This personal self is a total fantasy. It is a paradox. We are born into the dream play and we play our role as a character in the play. This character is animated by the force of Divine Energy. Everything is animated by it. The individual persona is a myth – a very short myth – something analogous to the cartoon character *Roger Rabbit.* When the movie is over, he erases himself and no longer exists. His character is taken out of form when he no longer has a role in the movie. Like this movie, we become a character in our own dream play until we exit the stage. At that point, the character ceases to exist but the universal Self lives on.

In other words, one can look at life as a type of animated movie. We come into the movie, play our role and leave. Popular belief will tell you that at this point the individual dies. However, many great sages and thinkers will tell us that this is the point where our true life begins.

At the point of dissolution of form, all concerns of the character played in the dream state no longer exist. Isn't this a great relief? It is something like a Shakespearean play where the actor who plays Brutus kills Caesar. Caesar is then removed from the drama and takes off his costume.

Similarly, our persona, when exiting this human life, leaves behind all aspects and characteristics held in the drama. You are spirit living the mortal dream. Instead of being a person in the cosmos, you are the cosmos.

As Shakespeare has so elegantly said:

*"All the world's a stage,*
*And all the men and women merely players.*
*They have their exits and their entrances,*
*And one man in his time plays many parts."*

*"The fundamental delusion of humanity is to suppose I am here and you are out there."*
--Yasu Tani Roshi

*One of the hardest tasks for the human mind to carry out is to become capable of seeing the whole of the drama of life as a movie that is being directed toward a particular end and to see the entirety as a purpose of demonstration effort, with the intent of teaching a lasting lesson for the benefit of all. Everything is under control, no matter how it looks. Manifest life is a theater in which the same results repeat themselves in ever evolving variations on a theme. Shakespeare illustrated this in myriad ways, as tragedy and*

*farce. The events and conditions that recycle here over and over, are all filtered through the lens of a given age.*
   –Les Visible, the "Dog Poet"

As Robert Adams states: *"All is well. There are no mistakes. Everything is unfolding as it should."*

*"The fairest thing we can experience is the mysterious. It is the fundamental emotion which stands at the cradle of true art and true science."*
  --Einstein

*"Our separation from each other is an optical illusion."*
  --Einstein

# Chapter 1 - Nothing is the Way it Seems

When you look in a mirror, what do you see?

That depends on many factors, including language and interpretation. A scientist might see the light reflecting off a surface, showing an image of what is commonly called a human body. A celebrity might see symptoms of aging with rising fear of unpopularity. A young man might see a handsome face, hopefully appealing to others.

But none of these interpretations are who you really are. The question, "Who am I?" has been asked since the beginning of time. There are seminars and retreats where participants ask themselves this question continuously of one another for many days.

At first, you might be tempted to say, "I'm a father, or mother, or husband, or son, or teacher, etc." But are these not just labels?

What you see in the mirror depends on how you have been conditioned; it depends on your belief systems about who you are. But who are you really? Is the self you seem to experience in this life real at all?

## The Dream Analogy

Many mystics and sages have compared our life to a dream state, in no way more significant than a night dream.

In a night dream all the characters appear to be real, the settings are defined and clear, and the emotions felt seem like our own. You might have no idea that you are just dreaming as you move from plot to plot. While in this dream state you may experience total bliss because something favorable happens to your dream character. On the other hand you might experience excruciating horror or pain. Have you ever awakened from a dream totally terrified and then are so relieved to understand that it was just a dream and you are safe in the confines of your own home?

While in the dream there is no question of its validity – you believe in the contents of the dream as it unfolds from scene to scene. There can be many people in your night dream, all with personalities, characters, customs, and roles. But where are these people in reality?

We are so sure the dream is actually happening that in fact we have no idea that we are dreaming until we awaken (unless we become "lucid" within the dream. In such case, it is possible to become aware that we are dreaming while the story is still unfolding). But in most cases, as the passing dream ends it becomes obvious that the contents of it hold no basis in what we call our "real" lives. Whatever terror or joy was experienced in the dream evaporates into the morning air; the feelings experienced end as the dream ends.

We discover almost a duplication of the dream state in our everyday waking "reality," but most would not take their daily lives to be a dream because, as in the nightly dream state, they perceive their waking lives to be totally real. Just as the dreamer thinks that the dream world is real until he is awakened, so it is in the drama of our waking lives. What we consider to be our real existence involves a similar drama to the nightly dream.

As in the night dream, we totally identify with being the character that we are playing in the worldly drama of waking life. There is no question in most people's minds that they exist as individual human beings and their daily life is reality.

## The Night Dream Analogy – The Dream within the Dream

We are going to suggest that just possibly what we call "reality" is still a dream, and the night dream could be considered a dream within a dream. We go from the sleeping dream to the waking dream. What we consider to be our real existence is no more real than the nightly dream.

In what we call our daily lives, we see patterns that are almost a duplication of the dream state. The only difference is that the night dream state appears to be shorter. A night dream lasts minutes whereas our daily lives are perceived to be much longer. However, keep in mind that in linear time the universe is considered to be about 14 billion years old. Our life as we perceive it is just a passing moment in cosmic time, a bit like a shooting star. Yet we often take that short duration experience to be our sole identity.

Nothing is as it appears to be. The worldly dream is no more real than the night dream and at a certain point we will wake up from the mortal day dream and enter our true nature. As is so aptly put by many great teachers, you are not your body. You are not a mere human being. You are the absolute, omniscient, immortal and all loving perfection of the Divine, and as a Divine being, you are living the mortal dream.

The implications of this Divinity are vast. Essentially, when you awaken from the dream of daily life, you no longer live with the idea that your body will ultimately die, because the Divine is eternal – birthless and deathless.

## The Movie Analogy

This illusory dream world we call human life can be viewed as a feature movie with characters, customs, settings and dialogue.

Imagine you are watching a movie in a theatre at your local cinema. You decide you don't like the plot, so in the middle of the movie, you run up to the front of the theatre and start trying to rearrange the characters on the screen. Yet this is precisely how most people respond to the movie called "earthly life."

How real is the drama being played out on the screen? Did that scene really happen, or is it simply being projected onto the screen by the light of the projector as the film moves through it frame by frame?

Think of your mind as the projector, and your "life experience" as the film. The screen represents your daily life, with its activities and events. You cannot force your drama to change by attempting to rearrange the characters and events. Instead, you must find out who or what the projector is, or rather, who is running the projector.

When the movie is over and you leave the theatre, you return to the life you had prior to watching the movie, but when you are immersed in the movie, you temporarily forget the life you had before entering.

## The Nature of the Play

The word "persona" comes from the Greek word "mask." Each person is a character in the play of humanity wearing the mask of self-identity. The main character (or star) is what we call "I" or "me." The other characters, as well as the "I" or "me" in the dream play, are activated or charged into being by the ultimate "One." (Note: This key concept will be repeated often throughout the book.)

You can call the ultimate One anything you want: The Force, Allah, Jesus, Hasham, Mother Earth, the Great Spirit, the I AM Presence, etc. You can even use the scientific idea that this force is an electricity of sorts. It doesn't matter what we name this Divine energy; it is the power that lives and animates each of our dream characters.

At any given moment, the person immersed in the drama will think that he is manifesting the activities in the life he is playing, but in reality, the individual he calls "I" does not exist as a separate entity.

When the average person looks in the mirror, he identifies the image as himself. Usually, it takes someone who has dismantled all his programming and conditioning to be able to see that image as simply a projection and not himself. In other words, he is no longer identified with the ego.

As we stated, all the events in the drama are happening to your dream character, and like a night dream, your character will eventually awaken to its true identity and leave behind the person they played in the human drama. It is all an illusory world where we think we are individuals, but in actuality the drama is nothing more than the immutable presence of the Divine force wearing the many masks in the drama.

*Waking up in the twentieth century is quite complex and at the same time totally simple....We wake in the morning, put on appropriate apparel, eat to keep the body strong and functioning, stuff our purses or wallets with our identification stating exactly who we are, and walk off to the missions of our planned day. At work or along the way we are bombarded with all the threats coming from the media: huge natural events devastating thousands upon thousands; the latest mass murders; the slaughter or torture of health workers, animal protectors, etc. ALL these morbid events are for some the primary and most significant news of the world. The news spreads a subliminal fear, anxiety, apprehension, etc., into the air and into our psyche."*

--Paramahansa Yogananda

As Yogananda states, *"We must behave with detachment, realizing we are only actors or observers in God's cosmic movie."*

Those able to adopt the understanding that they do not exist as defined by society in the dream play, seem to be giving up a lot…but ultimately what replaces the ego is free observation of the events in your character's life with an understanding that the pain, horror, and ultimate death, as well as the joy, love, and good times, are all part of the passing illusion.

*"Most of us recognized ourselves in the mirror this morning. The person looking back at us has a familiar name, a family, a job. He (or she) carries around a long menu of likes and dislikes, along with a personal history from the moment we emerged from the womb. It would*

*amaze the vast majority of the human race to be told that this person in the mirror is an illusion."*
　--Deepak Chopra

## More on the Movie Analogy

There are many analogies being made regarding the movie-like nature of the mind. Earlier we described one such system with the mind as the movie projector, the film as life experience, and the movie screen as the actions of daily life.

We illustrated the absurdity of attempting to change the movie by running up to the front of the theatre and trying to forcefully move the characters around on the screen as the movie is playing. At the very least, you would get an angry response from the audience, and you might even get locked up for insane behavior.

Yet that is precisely what you are doing if you are trying to change people and situations in life without changing your consciousness.

You see the world that your consciousness shows you, because you are not separate from the world, just as the movie is not separate from the projector. The mind is the perceptive mechanism, and that is a good definition for the mind. The mind allows you to see a projection of its internal reality on the outer stage of life.

## Comparing Life to a Hologram

In the science section of this book, there will be factual evidence for the claims being made herein. One of these, the holographic model of the universe, suggests that everything you perceive is a projection from beyond the screen of life. Holograms are three-dimensional projections from a flat surface and begin as a whole and are then reduced down into a series of smaller "wholes." The dreams generated by the subconscious mind while the body is asleep are similar in that they appear real, with depth, color (for most dreamers) and a story line.

Could it be that the waking dream is a holographic projection in much the same way as the sleeping dream? The most significant difference is that the waking dream seems to have a collective perception that is lacking in the sleeping dream. However, there are cases where sleeping dreams have been "shared" by different dreamers, indicating that there is a potential connection between dreamers. Many scientists also suggest that the dream state is common to, or actually exists, as a projection within the collective mind of humanity, or even the universal mind, which is said to span various dimensions of time and space.

A related idea is that mind itself is shared, similar to the manner in which Carl Jung described – a collective unconscious or "race mind."

Perhaps to answer the questions about dreams, it is important to look at the idea of mind itself.

## What is the Mind and Where is it Located?

Human beings have experienced severe brain damage, where huge sections of the brain have become inoperable, and yet the brain-damaged human is able to function, in many cases, as if the damaged sections were intact. This suggests that the various centers of the brain are not the actual centers of consciousness, but rather, just relay stations that process, transmit and receive signals from a source located outside the material regions of the brain.

Research suggests that the mind is an intelligent field of energy that surrounds the physical brain and is in fact located in an alternate dimension of time and space. This alternate dimension is connected in ways that seem to violate the laws of everyday physics, just as the night dreams often seem to be outside such "normal" laws. Likewise, you are an intelligent field of energy and your Real Self is not located within the physical body, but exists outside the world of appearances.

It is possible to perceive the world without a separate self. However, we are encouraged to think of ourselves as individuals. Society reinforces the idea of individuality by constantly attempting to convince us that we need various products and services designed to improve our self-image.

Your thoughts of personal inadequacy become a distraction and prevent true communication with others. When you recognize the illusory nature of your thoughts, it is easier to align with your Divine Presence.

At this point, we can release our core belief system that all objects and surroundings are separate from us or outside us. We no longer identify with the body's senses or mind and we end the perception of a separate world of "you" and "me."

To sum up this main point, the personal self is a total fantasy. We are born into the dream play and this character is fabricated by our beliefs. The illusory self is merely an animation of Divine energy.

The Nature of the Dream Character

Again, due to the importance of this key concept, the initial premise will now be stated in a slightly different manner.

At birth we are born into the dream play as a reflection or extension of the Divine. At this infant stage our true identity is usually not revealed to us. We live in complete innocence or beingness until approximately the age of two. Our Real Self, which reflects our Divine nature, is covered up by programming. We are given a name; the character that we are to play is rehearsed; and slowly we become educated to the morals, mores, standards and expectations of the family into which the dream character is born.

The conditioning or training to play this role creates in the guileless a complete identity. This identity constructs an imaginary self, or as Eckhart Tolle describes, a phantom self. The beingness or Divinity of the individual is usually completely repressed. The phantom self now lives out its life according to the restrictions imposed on the character. The toddler is indoctrinated to consider everything as separate from himself (his character).

Hence, hatred for different cultures and religions is often part of the separation program. This is why world history shows such a war-like and divisive drama. A competitiveness is generated that creates a great sense of separation and stirs up the idea that this imaginary self must fight for survival and a sense of superiority. Without this sense of separation, we would likely grow up in a world of peace and harmony.

A character in the dream play may be born as a woman in Iraq, conditioned to believe and honor the standards of her culture, (i.e., given a script and role in the play) while the woman born into a family in Beverly Hills is indoctrinated with a whole different set of standards.

The ego, or the identification with the imaginary self, will follow the dream character for his entire lifetime.

Our whole quality of life is rendered by our level of attachment to the dream character. All the thoughts, loves, prejudices, hatreds, and preferences take control and this ego conditioning becomes the basis of belief. Our belief systems take control of our thoughts.

From the phantom self thoughts are generated, based on conditioning. These thoughts control the character. Emotions are then based on these thoughts.

It is difficult to believe that one's entire perception of reality is based on a false premise. We come into this illusory world as clear and innocent beings and slowly we are given a script and are programmed to believe whatever our parents and others taught us to think is reality.

The toddler perceives, "Everyone is calling me so and so; therefore I am so and so." He becomes identified with his name; a simple word. This is the prelude to a storm that is going to engulf the actor as he plays out his identity (role).

The characteristics of the persona go on and on…. I am tall or short, intelligent or stupid, cute or ugly, and I have a certain religion and belief system. The storm of identity continues to implode into the character's script.

We adopt positive and negative attitudes. A world view is implemented. This includes taking on understandings of the world around us that are destructive or dangerous.

It is a given fact that the persona of the toddler is distinct and separate from every other persona – an autonomous individual with a coherent identity and sense of free will. This is an illusion. Illusions are experiences that seem real only because you believe in them.

All of this conditioning prepares the actor for his role on the stage of the theatre of life. He enters the drama at birth and lives out his roles as defined by his script (belief systems and conditioning).

To summarize, it is most important to understand that the existence of the persona is an illusion. The imaginary self is a fabrication from memory and conditioning. This illusion does not exist independently of the person having the experience.

Here is the very good news: Michael Jeffreys says,

*"You can't get out of the dream because you were never in the dream. The dream is for the dream character, the 'action figure,' not you. If you are what is seeing the movie, then you will know that you are not the movie. Even if a character dies in the movie, what does it have to do with you? Nothing. There's nobody, no separate entity, and there never has been."*

## Recognizing Our Divine Self

To be free you must recognize that the imaginary character you personify or are conditioned to believe in, is not who you really are. Your Divine Self or Beingness is your true nature.

Let us repeat something we said earlier, this time with emphasis:

**It is commonly believed that we are mortal beings created by the Divine, but in actuality we are the Divine living the mortal dream.**

If the actor in the play of life discovers his oneness with all other actors he will be moved to help other forms, not destroy them.

Can you see how releasing your identification with the little self will alleviate wars and hatred among nations, and bring peace to humanity?

The feeling of being you comes from consciousness; the undivided whole of awareness. It is an incredible paradox. The feeling that you exist is not coming from a separate self, even though the mind interprets it this way. **That inner feeling of existing is coming from a united whole consciousness. It is not coming from a separate entity called "you" because there is no "you."**

With this new way of looking at the human drama, the character who is experiencing the drama dissolves.

*The illusory dream world can be viewed as a feature movie with characters, customs, settings and dialogue. One's values are profoundly changed when one is finally convinced that creation is only a vast movie and that not in it, but beyond it, lies one's own reality (consciousness).*

--Paramahansa Yogananda

*"As long as you believe you are the body-mind phenomena you're going to have problems. You may feel justified in having problems. You may feel it's not your fault. You may feel it's karmic. You may feel all kinds of things, but as long as you believe or you feel the body-mind, you will have problems, because this is the kind of world in which we live – a world that doesn't exist seems real to most of us. And if we believe we are the body-mind*

*then we believe the world is real and we believe we have to pray to God for solutions. We do all these things and we still suffer. And suffering will only stop, not when God answers your prayers, but when you awaken to the truth of your own being. Then you're born again, so-to-speak, in a new reality and all is well."*

--Robert Adams

*Q: Why do not worldly men give up everything to find God?*
*A: Can an actor coming on the stage throw off his mask at once? Let worldly men play out their part, and in time they will throw off their false appearance.*

--Sri Ramakrishna

# Chapter 2 – The Drama of Life

The very nature of the dream play is emptiness. Einstein, in his famous equation $E=mc^2$ concludes that 99.99 percent of everything is empty space. We are so conditioned to see everything as solid. To embrace Einstein's theory takes a truly evolved human being. Because we are conditioned habitually to see everything as solid, one does not realize that we are truly not separate from other forms.

Democritus further reiterates that the first principle of the universe consists of atoms and empty space.

You might ask why you can't walk through a door if it is empty space. Apparently, according to Einstein's theories, you cannot penetrate another form with your form even if both are empty space. The reason for this is that the atoms of the one form repel the atoms of the other form.

If we could really grasp atomic principle, it would transport us to a true understanding of the nature of our dream world. Your form and every other form exists like a silhouette. When you pass out of form into the eternal realms your .01% solids dissolve into infinity.

Emptiness is the absence of the inherent existence of phenomena. To say that things are empty is to say that the dependence on conditions and related parts is such that nothing can be independently established.

Emptiness teachings in Buddhism suggest that all phenomena are empty of their own nature and being.

Whatever is identified or characterized exists in name only. Therefore conventional existence in Buddhism is also called nominal existence. For example, a pear is produced dependent on clouds, water, sunlight, air, wind, seeds, etc. None of these things exist on their own. A pear is produced from what is considered to be non-pear elements. So that pear does not have its own nature. If the conditions that the pear depends upon would cease to exist, there would be no pear. A pear lacks its own being.

There is an invisible gaseous substance (mostly nitrogen and oxygen) connecting us, making us as one. The fact that this gas goes into and out of different bodies in no way implies that these bodies are separate. They are composed of liquids and solids, which are just different forms of energy.

To apply the theory of emptiness to the human condition, each form or persona is an image generated from energy vibrating in mostly empty space. Each individual is an animation of the Divine force. The individual assumes a character in the dream play or movie, with his own styles, beliefs, hates, loves and motivations. This is the character's story. And people define themselves by their stories. However, for you to truly believe that the sum total of your existence is the character you are playing, is burdensome and limiting because it denies your Divinity.

No matter how charming or beautiful your story is, it is still fiction. If you believe that your character and the story are real, you will never find inner peace or well-being.

Happiness will always be conditional, depending upon what the story is personifying. If you believe you are truly this character you will be thrust from joy to sorrow and back, depending upon the conditions that appear in your drama. Over and over, the character is plunged into self-doubt and conflict until the form is finally laid to rest.

In order to be free, one must identify not as a body but as the omnipresent Divine that manifests the persona. It takes focus, and removal (detachment) from our conditioning to identify the True Self as awareness. When we identify as awareness or consciousness we enter an alternate perspective, one that is not popularly recognized by society at large. It takes further introspection and the sublimation of the ego to understand and accept the fact that you are not the personal "I." It takes additional humbling of the ego to understand that any perception of control over the circumstances of your story is an illusion.

Similar to Einstein, Spinoza was a strict determinist who believed that human behavior (as well as the contents of your story) is completely predetermined. The only real choice we have is to accept or deny the reality that things are not the way they appear, and not give such appearances the power to destroy our feelings of well-being. In a moment, we will take a closer look at the subject of free will and predestiny.

Everything is merely thought to exist. Accordingly, the story you are living is already written (by your Divine Self) and you are simply animating it. Your character is suffering the dilemmas in your story, not you. For you are not this character – this imaginary self that you are conditioned to think you are. If you truly understand that you are not the body/mind phenomena, there's nothing else to do. Everything will appear in accordance with the Divine Plan – not your personal will. Most people live their drama endlessly going from one circumstance to another without understanding that they are not the doers. In essence they are being lived by Divine energy and this Divine Presence is making the decisions, not the little self.

In understanding that you are not the character in the dream play, you are released from bondage. There is bondage when you believe the world can do something to you, or turn you this way and that way. And you are in bondage when you take the world seriously.

You might be tempted to interject:

"Now how can I not worry about this world? Look at the dastardly things going on! Look at man's inhumanity to man, the wars we have, etc."

The only way out of the suffering that exists in the world today is for humanity to adopt an advanced perspective on reality. If we understand the laws of quantum physics thoroughly, we will know that we are all connected and animated as One.

Dr. David Bohm and J. Krishnamurti determined that consciousness projects itself outward as thought, and thought is a material process that gives rise to the concept of a material world "out there" separate from the perceiver.

In truth, the perceiver and the perceived are One. The observer is the observed. Think about this for a moment. If everything we see is our One Self, then why would we want to hurt ourselves? Rather, we would want to relieve our own pain, whether it is in our own body, or the body of another.

Perhaps you don't believe that there is no world "out there," but in Chapter 3, several branches of science are examined that point directly to this conclusion. Basically, we see the world that we want to see, or at least that we expect to see. In other words, beliefs create our perception of reality.

Metaphysics essentially states that the world is created by thought. You are advised that by changing your consciousness, you change your reality.

While consciousness itself might be beyond thought, the movement of consciousness in the form of thought can be measured as electrical impulses that go through the brain. In other words, thoughts are things. They are the stuff the dream world is made of. If you want to change the world, or the characters in the movie of your life, you must change the film in the projector (your thoughts, beliefs and programs).

Let us return to the idea that "we are our brother's keeper." Jesus said, "What you do to the least of your brethren, you do to me."

It appears Jesus had a unified consciousness. He did not see himself as separate from the so-called "outer" world or the people in it.

What we are hinting at is adopting a new perspective with which we can bring about **a peaceful revolution.** It is in having this new perspective and seeing everyone as our Self that we would automatically want to help rather than hurt, while at the same time surrendering to what is manifesting. By surrender, we mean accepting the "what is" of every moment, without judgment. Looking with complete neutrality upon the world removes us from the reactive mind and we are able to see clearly what action effects the maximum benefit on our "brethren."

To reiterate, what is going on in the world is illusory. At the moment it appears solid and real. However, going back to Einstein, it is almost all empty space. Once you become free of the personal ego, or "I," you will see the world in a new perspective. How could the happenings in human history be real if they are impermanent and passing? However, if we are unable to get beyond the illusory nature of existence and instead get caught in the feelings and suffering of our fellow man, it is at this point that we must remember that this is only a drama. Also, since everything is One, that means that another's pain is our own pain.

A person who is liberated, who has freed his or her mind of all mental afflictions, still experiences physical pain. The difference between us and an arhat, a person who has freed the mind from mental affliction, is that the arhat doesn't identify with the pain. Arhats experience the physical pain of self and others vividly but don't grasp onto it; they can take action to avoid or alleviate pain, but whether they do so or not, the physical pain doesn't become real for them.

Ramana Maharshi had an advanced case of cancer. When asked whether he was in pain, he replied, "There is pain." He did not own it. What an arhat does not experience is mental suffering.

A Buddha, one who is perfectly spiritually awakened, has gone a step further. A Buddha has no mental suffering of his own, but is vividly and non-dually aware of the suffering of others.

Superficially, the arhat who is free from mental suffering can seem to us, who lack this realization, as numb and detached, in a state of existential anesthesia. **A Buddha, one who is fully awakened, presents the paradox of being free from suffering and also non-dually present with other people's joys, sorrows, hopes and fears.** A Buddha taps into deep peace, the ultimate ground state of awareness beyond the dichotomy of stimulus-driven pain and pleasure. The mind of a Buddha has been purified of all obstruction and from his own being there naturally arises immutable bliss, like a spring welling up from the earth.

⊂⇒

*With the unveiling of the Buddha-nature of unconditional bliss, there is also a complete erosion of the absolute demarcation line between self and others. The barrier is gone. This is why the Buddha is vividly and non-dually aware of the suffering of others who are identified with their illusory beliefs, hopes and fears. The Buddha sees the whole situation, and at the same time is not disengaged from the purity and bliss of his own awareness. The mind of a Buddha doesn't block out anything and nothing is inhibited, and this is why the awareness of an awakened being is frequently described as "unimaginable."*

---B. Alan Wallace.

*"Empty things are born from empty things."*
– Nagarjuna.

Buddha, when asked to explain his enlightenment, said: *"A knot of empty space entwined with empty space has been untied."*

<u>Let us repeat because of its importance</u>: The story you are living is already written by the Divine and you are simply animating it. Your character is suffering the dilemmas in your story, not you. For you are not this character, this imaginary self that you are conditioned to think you are. Not your personal will, but thy will be done. In this case, "thy will" refers to your real Divine Self.

As stated previously, this new perspective can bring about a peaceful revolution. It is in adopting this new perspective and seeing everyone as One Self that we automatically want to help rather than hurt, while at the same time surrendering to what is manifesting in our lives and theirs. "Love your neighbor as yourself," takes on a clearer meaning and relevance because your neighbor *is* yourself.

It all comes around in a full circle, not as karma, but as an interconnectedness that affects everything in Creation.

Once you have begun the process of identifying with the Divine within you, or have realized that you are pure consciousness, you are able to leave your story behind. At this point you enter what some might call a magical world. With everything being seen as totally connected through yourself, you begin to live the beatific vision. The beatific vision comes to you from seeing everything as One. **The beatific vision is the state of rapturous bliss that arises when everything and everyone is seen as the face of the Divine.**

Finally, you are face to face with the expression of the Divine everywhere and in everyone. Most people identify the beatific vision as something that comes only to holy people rather than the common person. It is actually available to all of us because the Divine lives in all of us.

As we awaken from the dream, we see the Divine in each and every person, from the sinner to the saint, from the kind and generous to the mean and nasty. We stop reacting to the negativity of others and thus, stop reinforcing their bad behavior. We know that beneath the behavior is our One Self simply caught in the dream.

When the tie that binds is broken,
You return to your rightful place.
Beyond the dream that left you,
 Is a name without a face.
In the world you cling to,
That holds you in its spell,
You begin to question,
"Who am I?" but cannot tell.
You are the absolute,
You are the consciousness complete,
You've taken your ego to the One,
And laid it at his feet.
There is no tie that's broken.
You never left your rightful place.
Your dream was only borrowed,
By a name without a face.

Free Will and Predestiny

As promised, we are going into a bit more depth on the subjects of free will and predestiny, much misunderstood topics. As with everything else in life, understanding of this subject depends on your perspective. Let's use an illustration:

Imagine you are in a forest, walking on a trail. You can see a little ways behind you and a little ways in front of you. This path represents what you call "linear time" or past, present and future on the clock.

Now, suppose you climb a tall tree and look out across the forest. Down below you is the trail you have been walking on. Now, you can see where you have been and where you are going. This is the domain of linear time spread out below you, viewed from a dimension beyond linear time.

From this vantage point, it appears you have nearly unlimited choices available to you. You can remain on the path going forward. You can reverse your steps and go backward. Or, you can wander off the path and explore some other part of the forest.

However, from your vantage point, let's suppose you can see the entire forest. Therefore, you can see all possible paths that you think you can choose. In other words, the field of possibilities is predetermined, even though to the little illusory self it might seem to present an unlimited possibilities. The ego self can seem to choose path it desires, but it is restricted to the field of possibilities.

Since time and space are really part of the same dimension, the possibilities you seem to see involve time as well as space. Therefore, all time is laid out before you as well and you are viewing all time from this now moment while sitting up in the tree.

The ramifications of this are far-reaching. Although you seem to have choice regarding the order in which you explore the field of possibilities, as well as your emotional reactions to the experiences you have, you are still operating within a predetermined domain.

## The Real Self (Higher Self)

In this discourse so far, the author has spoken at length about Divine being or consciousness. Consciousness is everything. It is a mysterious power that continuously lives within us. It is the Real Self. Imagine that the person sitting in the tree looking out at the entire forest is your Real Self. What you call "I" in the story is simply a short lived image superimposed upon this power. The body can cry, laugh, and go through all sorts of experiences but your True Self, your awareness, which we call consciousness, is not affected. In truth, nobody is affected.

Imagine you are looking down from the treetop and there is a drama unfolding below you on the trail. From your vantage point, you are completely unaffected by this drama; it doesn't even involve you.

What's going on in your life is a program. There is nothing in this universe that can ever hurt your True Self. No matter how things appear and how they feel at first, they cannot hurt you because there is nothing that can be hurt. Everything that appears is temporary, including your life story. Consciousness is all there is. Nothing can destroy it *because* it is all there is.

It is a mystery why people take refuge in the outside world, in a person, place or thing, when we know the outside world is subject to the law of change. For example, the toddler becomes the old man. Things in this world never remain the same for long. Sometimes happy occurrences take place in the dream, and sometimes there are horrible things. When you identify with the world inevitably disappointments will come. Everything you grab in this world is like sand. It seems so real. Then your emotions take hold of it and give it more power so the experience becomes stronger. As the attachment to a desired outcome or experience grows, you become gripped in fear, frustration or doubt. You made these things real for you due to the power of your belief – in this case, the belief that certain things of this world will bring you happiness and fulfillment.

It takes an immense amount of humility to surrender to the idea that you are not a personal self; you must give up all the programs and beliefs that say this little self is you. **However, this change of perspective contains its own reward – total liberation from suffering.**

Once again, think of the false self as a person walking on the trail, and your Real Self as the field of consciousness watching from the treetop.

Giving Up Attachment and Fear

You cannot be mentally or emotionally attached to a person, place or thing and be awakened at the same time. If you want liberation, you have to pay the price and the price is letting go, giving it all up, surrendering all the appearances in the dream. This does not mean you must deprive yourself; only that you cannot identify with material things and find true happiness.

The human race has its fears. These fears are dependent on cultural conditioning. Fears arise over money, power, love, health, appearance. This list could go on and on. Liberation comes when you understand that you live at the mercy of the Force, the Divine being to which we all are a part. Being a part of the Divine Force extends to us the characteristics of this Force. With this as the truth, you become what you have always been – pure awareness – Omnipresent, Omnipotent and Omniscient.

You are so much more than you have been taught to believe you are. You are Atman. Atman is the innermost Self or spirit of humankind, but different than the empirical ego. The Atman is the ultimate reality behind all worldly objects and Atman is the pure spirit in all beings. Atman is the eternal, all pervading reality underlying all existence. The average man suffers in the grip of incessant desires and ignorance. Upon realization of the Self, one becomes free of the shackles of desires, aspirations and passions. This is liberation. If one reaches the state of Atman the body will do what it has to do in the world but it will not react to conditions. This state of liberation is experienced by only a few at the present time.

Look at yourself. Are you awake or are you asleep? I am the Self. You are the Self. The world/universe is the Self. There is nothing else. Everywhere you look you see your Self. Everything is unfolding exactly as determined by Divine Self.

## Your Identification, Please

The author agrees that almost all news and most occurrences in the world appear dismal; the realm of appearances is a horrific mess, with brutal deaths, starving masses, downtrodden women; and many greedy people trying to get more and more for themselves at the great expense and suffering of the so-called victims of society.

As stated earlier, all of this is a complete illusion. What we perceive as the drama of life is a fable. None of it truly exists and neither does the individual identity that we hold on to as a representation of who we are.

Take for example, John Doe, who lives at 31 Broadway, New York, New York. He's a lawyer, but this identification has nothing to do with the person so named. It is a fake identity assigned to a form in this worldly drama. It is not who he really is. Yet he totally believes this is who he is.

Perhaps you have a passport, or driver's license, or state-issued I.D. Do your body, emotions and mind depend on this card or paper document? Would you still have the same body and most of the same thoughts even if this document did not exist? Of course. Maybe it would be more difficult to travel and communicate with state authorities without your documents, but nobody with any level of sanity is going to equate the personal self with the documents. However, this is essentially what we are doing when we identify with the thoughts and beliefs of the little self. We are saying, "I am a lawyer, I am a wife or husband, I am a father or mother."

There is a way to find your true identity shining through the false identification that has formed a mental construct denying the Real Self of the person. The identity of John Doe is not the reflection he sees in the mirror. This reflection, if believed, will almost always bring much suffering to the persona. There is a way to look at the world situation and one's identity with magical joy. This different perspective sees John Doe as a non-existent identity; he is, rather, a life form completely connected to the Divine. He is a vehicle for the all-knowing Divine Self to express through him, even though he is living conceptually as a human being.

It is the author's intention to deconstruct the self-image of John Doe and bring this character to a more accurate understanding of his true identity.

To repeat, all the events in the drama are happening to dream characters. These characters in the play take off their costumes once the play is over (at death or Self-realization) and go back to the identity they had before – just like Caesar and Brutus.

It is all an illusory world where we think we are live individuals, but in actuality the drama is nothing more than the immutable presence of the Divine Force wearing the many masks in the drama.

The enlightened human can control his thoughts and quiet his mind to look at the beauty of a sunset or feel the love of a child or pet, but without identifying with what he sees. It is a paradox. **You are everything that you see and, at the same time, you are beyond everything you see.**

## Freedom from Denial

The understanding associated with true perception will bring with it a great liberation from the mortal dream; often with a feeling of joy, and a totally different perspective on the brutality we see in the world sphere. This is not to say that you become hardened or indifferent to the suffering. That is denial, avoidance or escape, and it is the false self that employs such tactics. By denying the occurrence of this false perception of self, you are perpetuating the drama. What you resist persists. **If you are refusing to look at the worldly drama, with all its suffering, agony and misery, then you are not free – you still believe in the reality of this world and are simply reacting to it by sticking your head in the sand.**

There are many so-called New Age teachers and students who are pretending that they have transcended the ego and are "above" and "beyond" the suffering. They are simply in denial. Denying the darkness is just as counter-productive as glorifying it and making it real. An enlightened being has great compassion for the suffering, because he knows he was once caught in the same net of illusion.

## The Nature of the Individual Persona

The concept of ego – the development of the personality from birth and early childhood, is a difficult one to let go of. After all, this is how the characters in the drama are created and maintained. You are taught to invest your entire life in this false self. At age two, the toddler is not thinking about whether or not this self is real – he is simply attending to the tasks at hand – such as learning to walk, talk and understand the basic things of this world. He has no concept of the programming and conditioning that is slowly solidifying the illusion (forming and modifying his character and attempting to make it real). Since he (and his parents and authority figures) believes in it, it is real for him.

One of the central points of Buddhist philosophy is the renunciation of the existence of a separate self. Life simply is. One is taught to be mindful, meaning to pay attention to the well-being of all creatures.

Those brought up in a spiritual environment might not attach to the ego as strongly as those in a materialistic culture, but the individual sense of self is still there. It has simply become more subtle, more cunning. Perhaps, if you are a spiritual person, you have a sense of superiority; that somehow you are better than those without a spiritual focus. Do not let yourself fall into this trap. This is still a form of attachment to the belief in separation, however lofty it might seem. After all, fear can be clothed in righteousness.

## Undoing the Ego

To begin unraveling your identification with the little self, ask the questions:

Where do I exist? In my hand, in my head? Where? You are pure energy and perhaps some of that energy exists in the infinite field that surrounds the physical form. This aspect of the field tends to identify with the form.

Your individual self has experiences of this world. And it is a product of those experiences. This is why everyone appears different. No two human beings are brought up exactly the same. If your dream character believes in reincarnation or life on other planets, you could argue that souls bring experiences with them into this life that they acquired somewhere else. Regardless of whether the programming and conditioning originated in this life, or somewhere else, the problem is the same – identification with the material form.

Even identical twins are not identical – at least from a worldly viewpoint. They might get similar treatment from parents and have largely identical experiences growing up, but they will not be the same. It is the nature of the dream world to have each illusory self be unique and different. Once you are free from identification with this world, you can appreciate the differences and contrasts between individual human beings, but you will not make the mistake of thinking that these separate selves are the truth.

Learn to undo the ego by recognizing its strategies and reactions. Every time you do something, or have a desire, ask yourself, "What is the true purpose of this activity or desire? What do I hope to accomplish by engaging in this task? What is the ultimate objective of this behavior?" If the purpose of a thought, idea or behavior is to protect the little self, or make it bigger, or exalt it in some way, learn to recognize this and let it go. Recognition is the first step. Next, remember that you are the Divine Self watching the movie. In other words, stop identifying with the strategy and constant plans of the ego. See the false nature of these endless plans. See the illusory beliefs behind the plans. Recognize the attempts to prop up the "me" or "I," to make it more important or ensure its safety.

## Identification with Material Form

As we have explained previously, the character in the drama is formed through programming and conditioning. Every memory and sense of continuity of the personal self is a product of the experiences that that character has been through. The more intense experiences, and those that are repeated regularly, engender programmed responses. These are habit patterns. Your ego self is a product of your environment, your conditioning, the church, the schools you have attended, etc., and you develop certain habits of response and engagement. This is your script.

You have a predictable, programmed reaction to certain things in your life, such as an aversion to some types of people, obsessions and compulsions, reactions toward certain behaviors – for example, racial profiling of people, prejudices, etc. Liberation cannot occur until you are able to step beyond these habitual ways of thinking and feeling.

You can test yourself right now. Imagine someone is criticizing you unfairly, or attempting to make your life miserable in some way. What do you say in response? How do you feel? Be honest. It might be obvious, but in order to get to where you want to be, you must start where you are. Start with being honest about the degree of programming and conditioning you are still subject to at this point in your journey. How real are you making the dream world? How strongly do you believe in it? Are you reacting, rather than responding to life?

Notice also your self-judgment. Are you judging the way you think and feel? Are you making yourself wrong? Doing this sets up an inner conflict between "what is" and "what should be." You have created a split within the illusory self that keeps you divided and attached to the illusion. You have a program or belief about the way you think you should be feeling, and the feelings you are having are not in alignment with that program or belief, and so you react to your reaction. This perpetuates the illusion.

In later chapters, we will talk about some specific things you can do to disengage from the world of illusions. In the meantime, we encourage you to take a look at the scientific basis for the ideas presented in this book. Not all readers need scientific proof of what the author is saying, but there are many that will likely benefit from this approach. Before we begin the science section, let's leave you with a couple of quotes:

*"When you become involved in your thoughts about yourself, you are involved with the false self; when you are not, you drop into the pure experience of the moment. The sense of "I" drops away and you become the universe. When you let yourself be nothing, you realize yourself as everything. These are two very different ways of being!"*
–from Love and Surrender, part of The Jesus Trilogy

*"If you say, 'I am feeling sad,' doesn't that imply two entities? If so – who is this mysterious observer and who is the 'I'? If there is a subject (an observer) and an object (the observed), which one are 'you'? Are you the observer or the observed? Perhaps you are the observer but have confused yourself with what is being observed! .... Maybe 'I' is an idea....A thought, an illusion, a dream. Perhaps it's time to wake up from that dream?"*
--Tony Parsons

# Chapter 3 - The Science that Supports the Idea of a Dream World

There are many ideas from the world of science that back up the assertions made in this book. Below we have detailed a few related perceptions made by prominent physicists and philosophers.

Author Sal Rachele, in his book, "*Life On the Cutting Edge*," reminds us that we never see what is actually "there" in the material world:

"*Many religions teach that the physical world is an illusion. This is…true in the sense that what we see with the body's eyes is only an image of what is actually there. All we see is the reflected light from an object as it hits the retina of the eye, is recorded and interpreted by the brain, and is then transmitted via nerve impulses back to the optical faculties. Also, when we look at the physical world with our conventional senses, we see only the past. We do not see what is occurring now. Even this printed page (or computer screen) is being viewed in the past. It takes light reflected from this page one or two nanoseconds to reach the retina of the eye, etc.*"

It's like looking in a mirror. The image you see is not really there – it's just a reflection. Everything you think you see out in the world is merely a reflection of light being recorded by the brain. Based on the reflection of light, there is no proof that there is an outside world at all.

In other words, the idea that we are looking at reality, at what is really there, is completely erroneous.

Mr. Rachele goes on to reiterate what Einstein and many others have stated:

*"In addition to the time lag involved in physical perception, there is also the illusion of solidity in material objects. The atoms that make up physical matter are like tiny solar systems floating in a vast space. The speed at which the electrons orbit the atomic nucleus gives the appearance of solidity. The sheer number of atoms in an object also contributes to this illusion. Actually, there is far more "space" than atomic substance. Most objects are more than 99.99% empty 'space.'"*

Hence, based on our perceptions, we have been taught by traditional science that we feel and sense solid objects existing separately from our being. Isaac Newton's laws of motion, thermodynamics, etc., have been accepted by almost everyone. They give us a predictable behavior of the universe in everyday life situations, but that does not mean that what we perceive is reality.

Finally, we are given the analogy of the light spectrum to prove beyond a doubt that the "spiritual" universe is infinitely larger than the "physical" universe:

## The Light Spectrum

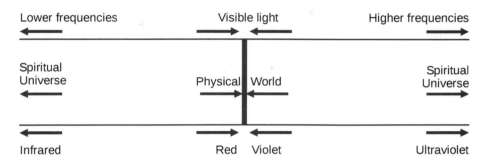

*"We hear of the larger 'spiritual' universe that exists beyond the physical one. A definition of 'spiritual' is 'That which exists in the invisible.' Both science and religion acknowledge the existence of this vast realm. For example, if you have ever seen a chart of the light spectrum, you know that the visible part is only a tiny line between infrared and ultraviolet. All the beauty of this world, as well as the billions of stars in the night sky, are represented by this tiny line on the light spectrum. Although we can measure some of the frequencies beyond our physical senses, these frequencies are invisible to us and hence, by definition, are part of the infinitely larger spiritual universe."*

--Sal Rachele

If what we experience in everyday life is real, then it is a tiny portion of the overall reality. However, as we shall soon demonstrate, the idea that there is any "outer" reality at all appears to be erroneous.

Not only are we potentially seeing only 0.01% of what is there, but we are only using 5 to 10 percent of our brain in order to interpret it. This means that even if we were able to perceive truly what is "out there," we would have a difficult time fully comprehending its meaning.

## Quantum Entanglement and the Non-Locality Principle

First demonstrated in a laboratory in 1935 by Einstein, Podolsky and Rosen, and later reproduced by Dr. John Bell in 1964, these scientists were able to demonstrate that when you separate aspects of a particle in time and space, and then make changes to one of the aspects, the change registers in the other aspect instantaneously, regardless of the distance separating the aspects.

The principle of quantum entanglement suggests that information can be exchanged between objects at any distance throughout space/time without regard for traditional Newtonian mechanics or even Einstein's physics. In other words, objects are capable of communicating with each other instantaneously, without regard for the speed of light or any other apparent constraints.

In order for this to be possible, it has been suggested that there are higher dimensions, space/time warps or wormholes through which information can flow. However, regardless of the mechanics of entanglement, this idea implies that everything is connected, no matter how far apart aspects of it appear to be. This has spiritual overtones, and brings us to a very closely related idea, that of non-locality. If you follow the Non-Locality Principle to its logical conclusion (by studying the science behind this idea), it means there is an over-arching dimension beyond time and space from which all time and space originates. The implications of this principle are staggering. In order to fully appreciate what has been discovered by quantum physicists in the laboratory, let us summarize the main ideas derived from this principle:

- The observer IS the observed.

- There is no separation of time and space. They are both contained within a single point (singularity) having no mass. In other words, both time and space are illusions.

- Everything originates from this single point. (This is another way of describing the Big Bang.)

- There is a point within each one of us that is the EXACT SAME POINT. Not just similar, or in concert with, but the very same point. In fact, we are holographic projections of this single point, each projected out into the illusion of space/time in a unique fashion.

The Non-Locality Principle essentially proves the existence of God, although most physicists would certainly not describe it in these terms. However, the author describes it as One Being, or one intelligence, looking out through the eyes of billions of human beings (and perhaps beings in other worlds). Therefore, this principle challenges the idea that we exist as individual beings separate from each other and the universe.

Here are a few brief observations from scientists involved with non-locality in the laboratory:

Dr. John Hagelin says:
*"At the core, at the foundation of the universe is a single field of energy, a unified field, a single unified field of intelligence..."*

Nikola Tesla said:
*"My brain is only a receiver. In the universe there is a core from which we receive all knowledge, strength and inspiration."*

*There is evidence that our world and everything in it...are only ghostly images, projections from a level of*

*reality so far beyond our own that it is literally beyond both space and time."*
--Michael Talbot

*"Nonlocality suggests that the universe is in fact profoundly different from our habitual understanding of it, and that the 'separate' parts of the universe are actually potentially connected in an intimate and immediate way."*
--From "Physics of the Universe," by Luke Mastin, 2009.

Mastin goes on to say:
*"Nonlocality occurs due to the phenomenon of entanglement, whereby particles that interact with each other become permanently correlated, or dependent on each other's states and properties, to the extent that they **effectively lose their individuality and in many ways behave as a single entity**. The two concepts of nonlocality and entanglement go very much hand in hand, and, peculiar though they may be, they are facts of quantum systems which have been repeatedly demonstrated in laboratory experiments."*

Scientifically, the Non-Locality Principle has an immense implication that will eventually change the understanding of the mass consciousness. What has been discovered by quantum physicists in the laboratory is that the observer is the observed. There is no separation in time and space. Both are illusions.

The world of quantum physics shows that things are radically different from the way we have been taught to perceive them in everyday life.

Very shortly, the author will examine the work of another contemporary scientist that gives rise to this idea that everything originates from a single point. To repeat, there is a point in each illusory character of the dream play that is the exact same point...not just similar but the very same point. It is a fact that we are living in a holographic projection of this single point. Let's look at an example of non-locality as it pertains to the human body.

## The Non-Locality of the Human Mind

Earlier it was stated that human beings that have experienced extreme brain damage to certain parts of the brain are often still able to function as if the damaged areas were intact. This suggests that the various centers in the brain are not the actual centers of consciousness but rather, relay stations that process, transmit and receive signals from a source located outside the material regions of the brain.

An analogy would be that of a radio receiver and the radio waves that carry the voices of musicians and announcers. It would be foolish to open the radio and look through the wiring and components for the announcer or musicians that are playing. Likewise, it is erroneous to expect that the source of consciousness would be contained in the brain.

Earlier we asked the question, "Who am I?" and also, "Where am I?" It would be ridiculous to cut open the body looking for the "I." Is it contained in the head? In the fingers? How about the toes? Is the "I" an energy field? Is the whole concept of inner and outer reality based on actual existence?

As we stated earlier, research suggests that the mind is an intelligent field of energy that perhaps surrounds the physical brain and in fact is located in an alternate dimension of time and space or possibly beyond time and space altogether. This alternate dimension is connected in ways that seem to violate the laws of Newtonian physics, just as the night dreams often seem to be outside such "normal" laws.

Likewise, the Non-Locality Principle, which appears to defy Einstein's theories, suggests that there is a higher dimension penetrating and surrounding what we call the physical universe, and of course, the physical "I."

## Further Scientific Proof of the Illusion of the Drama

Now, we will give some more scientific references that support our basic theory that this world is an illusion.

Some metaphysicians have given models of a multidimensional universe that is remarkably similar to the multiple dimensions of superstring theory and other branches of theoretical physics.

The main concept of superstring theory is that everything is vibration; everything is energy. Many scientists talk of "affinities" or "resonant fields." Is this not unlike the concept of human relationships? Where do I end and you begin? We erroneously believe it is defined by the physical body, but science has shown that there is an electromagnetic field around the physical body, just as there is a field of consciousness around the brain.

So then, what exactly is consciousness? Who is it that is aware? Who is the watcher? Who is the "I?" To answer those questions, we will look at physics, metaphysics, philosophy and common sense. Fortunately, we have many seers and visionaries in the above disciplines to draw from.

*"We cannot be an observer isolating ourselves from the universe in our analysis of it all - simply because we are part of it all.*

*If quantum mechanics hasn't profoundly shocked you, you haven't understood it yet. Everything we call real is made of things that cannot be regarded as real."*
– Niels Bohr

## The Bose-Einstein Condensate and Emptiness

*"A Bose-Einstein condensate is a group of atoms cooled to within a hair of* <u>absolute zero temperature</u>*. When they are cooled to that temperature the atoms are hardly moving relative to each other; they have almost no free energy to do so. At that point, the atoms begin to clump together, and enter the same energy states. They become identical, from a physical point of view, and the whole group starts behaving* **as though it were a single atom.*"* (emphasis added)

--Jesse Emspak, from LiveScience.com

There are many implications of the Bose-Einstein condensate. Several top scientists are saying that the universe started out in a static state (at absolute zero temperature), meaning no movement whatsoever. Think of a timeless, eternal state of pure beingness, a single point of consciousness. Everything was "congealed" into a primordial "soup." Doesn't this sound remarkably similar to what is now called the "unified field?"

This principle implies that it takes energy to separate the primordial mass into individual protons, electrons and other particles. Where does this energy come from? If there is nothing external to the field (and there cannot be if the temperature is at absolute zero), then what brought the universe into being? What started the Big Bang? There had to be a source of essentially infinite energy present somewhere that caused the single point of condensate to expand into what we experience today. In other words, there had to be a field of energy outside the realm of time and space in order to give birth to the universe as we know it.

Science cannot solve the ultimate mystery of nature. And that is because, in the final analysis, we ourselves are part of the mystery that we are trying to solve.

Nevertheless, there are a few more points that science has contributed to our understanding of who we are, so let us continue.

## Everything is Energy

At the turn of the nineteenth century, a few physicists started to explore the relationship between energy and the structure of matter. In doing so, the belief that a physical, Newtonian material universe (that was at the very heart of scientific knowing) was dropped, and the realization that matter is nothing but an illusion replaced it. These scientists began to recognize that everything in the universe is made out of energy.

The ideas of this renegade group were not accepted by the mainstream until well into the 20th century. Now, in the 21st century, their discoveries are once again being studied.

*"Space is just a construct that gives the illusion that there are separate objects"*
--From a quantum physics journal.

It has been written about, over and over again, but cannot be emphasized enough. The world of quantum physics is an eerie one, one that sheds light on the truth about our world in ways that challenge the existing framework of accepted knowledge.

What we perceive as our physical material world, is really not physical or material at all; in fact, it is far from it. This has been proven time and time again by multiple Nobel Prize winning physicists (among many other scientists around the world), one of them being Niels Bohr, a Danish physicist who made significant contributions to understanding atomic structure and quantum theory.

Another prominent scientist, Dr. Heisenberg, also contributed to the modern realization that everything is energy. He is most famous for the "Uncertainty Principle" based on the double-slit experiment, the most well-known experiment in the history of modern science.

You might recall the double-slit experiment that proves energy can take the form of waves or particles, depending on whether or not they are observed.

The metaphysical idea derived from the double-slit experiment is that life is full of infinite possibilities until you focus on a desired outcome. At that point, the waveform "collapses" into a dominant timeline.

Put in lay person's terms, we see the world we expect to see. **The world seems real because we believe it is real.**

## The Holographic Universe

There is the holographic model of the universe that suggests that everything is a hologram projected from a single point. We have already stated that the illusory nature of the world is manifested out of the emptiness of space. Now let us look at science that backs up this idea.

There are numerous books and articles that portray the universe as a holographic projection.

There are a couple of attributes of holograms that you should be familiar with. The first is that they are three-dimensional projections from a two-dimensional space (using lasers and special mediums to give the appearance of depth in a flat surface). You can project an image of something and, with proper lighting, it will look real and solid.

Another attribute involves the simple idea that the whole is contained within the parts of a system. In other words, in a holographic universe, you can break the macrocosmic components of space and time down into smaller "pieces," each of which contains the information of the whole system. Think of a very big universe that breaks into smaller versions of itself, each complete in every respect. A simple analogy would be a large painting that is reproduced into smaller and smaller sizes, even finding its way onto postcards and even business ca

The human body is a hologram. Within the trillions cells in the average human form, there are solar systems of atoms and molecules that resemble the macrocosmic structure of solar systems, galaxies, star clusters and other large-scale phenomena.

Dr. Nassim Harimein has suggested that the whole structure and all the information about the entire universe can be found in a single proton.

What do today's scientists have to say about the idea that what we call "reality" is merely a holographic projection?

In the movie, "Holographic Universe," scientist Frederick Vester notes:
https://www.youtube.com/watch?v=QuANDlrTHyI

*"The statements of some scientists, that 'man is an image, everything experienced is temporary and deceptive and this universe is a shadow,' seems to be proven by scientists in our day."*

Everything we see, feel, taste, smell or touch – our entire perception of the universe, is merely electrical signals inside the brain. Essentially, the "external" world is a construct of our own consciousness.

*"Instead of you being inside the world you see, the world you see is inside of you."* – from "Holographic Universe."

to make the comparison
ıd so-called "waking" life.
*easily in an unreal world in our*
*an equally be true for the world*
*e waking dream]. When we wake*
uற ს *·e is no logical reason not to believe*
*that we have ა.. . ιtered a longer dream called 'real*
*life.'"*

Note: Only the first 15 minutes of this movie are relevant to our discussion. However, there is another movie of the same name: (https://www.youtube.com/watch?v=lMBt_yfGKpU) that features Dr. Amit Goswami, saying,

*"Our tendency is to think the world is out there, independent of our experience. It is not. Quantum physics has been very clear about this."*

The second movie goes on to say:
*"Many highly respected quantum physicists are telling us, based on the latest research, that we are living in a hologram, that our reality is a virtual image, that it is an illusion, it isn't real."*

Michael Talbot and David Bohm came up with the following:

*"Despite its apparent solidity, the universe is at heart a phantasm, a gigantic and splendidly detailed hologram....*

*What we call 'reality' is actually a holographic picture that only looks and feels real to those of us inside it."*

## The Work of Dr. David Bohm and J. Krishnamurti

Eastern philosopher, J. Krishnamurti met with renowned physicist, Dr. David Bohm, for a series of talks and discussions.

These two men had a series of meetings over 25 years on the nature of reality. It is difficult to distill the information down into a few paragraphs, but here is an attempt to do so.

Consciousness projects itself outward as thought, and thought is a material process that gives rise to the concept of a material world "out there" separate from the perceiver. While consciousness itself might be beyond thought, the movement of consciousness in the form of thought can be measured as electrical impulses that go through the brain.

It is well known that some people can influence objects with the mind. This can only be possible if sufficient energy is given to thought, in the form of intention, and then directed toward the object or outcome.

Taking the above concept that thoughts do not actually leave their source, it follows that in such cases of psychokinesis and telekinesis (the ability to move objects both near and at a distance without outside forces), the truth is that the perceiver becomes "part of" the object being perceived and is therefore able to move the object at will in a similar manner to the way a human being can move part of the body at will.

*"Our brain is the result of time, evolution. Our brain is not your brain and my brain, but the brain of mankind. This is difficult for you to see, and even recognize, because we have been so conditioned that it is my brain. And it is your brain."* – J. Krishnamurti

The above quote can be extended to include the entire universe. My brain and your brain are the brain of the universe. In fact, we *are* the universe.

*"When man becomes aware of the movement of his own thoughts, he will see the division between the thinker and thought, the observer and the observed, the experiencer and the experienced.* ***He will discover that this division is an illusion.****"* – J. Krishnamurti

The Work of Nassim Harimein

Well-known, eccentric physicist, Dr. Nassim Harimein, states that he has scientific evidence that we are all One. He has mathematical equations that describe a new unified field – of consciousness.

Dr. Harimein postulates that within every subatomic particle is a "black hole" or related anomaly that connects everything to a realm outside the normal concept of time and space. Think of every object in the universe being intimately connected to every other object through a wormhole-like link.

He also discovered that within the "space" between subatomic particles, which makes up 99.99% of everything in the universe, there is almost infinite energy.

The most important discovery he has made involves the measurements of a single proton within the nucleus of an atom. When calculated properly, he maintains that the mass/energy ratio of the proton, plus the "empty space" around the proton, is exactly equal to the mass of the entire universe. This essentially proves that within each proton is a hologram of the entire universe.

Within so-called "empty space" is the Source that connects everything. This fundamental energy is in everything, and is the Source of everything. This unified field work upholds the Non-Locality Principle of quantum physics, which basically states that within every atomic particle is the *exact same point*. There is truly no separation at all. Everything is a hologram of a single point, or singularity.

Dr. Harimein also states the importance of "going within" through meditation. In the still quiet mind is the singularity, the single point of Source that is in everything. There is no separation. The observer is the observed. Separation is an illusion.

You must have a unified consciousness to understand the significance of this. As long as you believe in a separate self, the "me" or "I", you cannot see the beauty and simplicity of life. People see what they expect to see, but that does not mean they are seeing the truth. The truth is in the stillness beyond ego.

Dr. Harimein's work can be found at http://www.theresonanceproject.org.

## The Work of Julian Barbour

British physicist Julian Barbour postulates that time and space are illusions and that what appears as movement is much the same as in film (movies). Reality consists of an infinite number of "stills" that are brought together by consciousness and organized in such a way as to give the illusion of movement. Since this movement is an illusion, time itself is also an illusion, according to Barbour.

Barbour argues that we live in a universe which has neither past nor future – a strange new world in which we are alive and dead in the same instant. (You might be aware of a dissertation called "Schrodinger's Cat" in which a cat exists in a quantum flux, when unobserved, implying that

the cat is both alive and dead at the same ti
https://en.wikipedia.org/wiki/Schr%C3%B6dinge
    In this eternal present, our sense of the
is nothing more than a giant cosmic illusion.

*"[I asked myself] how to reconcile the fact that the world seems to be classical, we seem to have a unique past, things seem to be in definite positions, and have a definite future — that's what it seems to be like, but quantum mechanics tells us that it is different — not like that at all."*
    --Julian Barbour

*"My basic idea is that time as such does not exist. There is no invisible river of time. But there are things that you could call instants of time, or 'Nows'. As we live, we seem to move through a succession of Nows, and the question is, what are they? They are arrangements of everything in the universe relative to each other in any moment, for example, now....*

*The interconnected totality becomes my basic thing, a Now. There are many such Nows, all different from each other. That's my ontology of the universe — there are Nows, nothing more, nothing less.*
    --Julian Barbour

## he Nature of Time

*"Can it be seen that the moment itself, THIS moment, as it is spontaneously and causelessly appearing, gives no indication, no evidence, no proof of a past moment having ever existed!? That ANY reference to a "past" comes 100% from a mind made mental overlay, i.e., a story about a fictional character in time, with a "past" and a "future," called "me."*
*The key to seeing this [thing called] time, is to look at the moment and LET IT TELL YOU whether or not IT is indicating ANYTHING about a past..."*
   --Michael Jeffreys

Perhaps you have seen those signs in taverns and bars, saying "Free beer tomorrow." How much beer do you think they have given away? Would they still be in business if they were constantly giving away their product? Show me where tomorrow is. I'll give you all my money, power, prestige, etc., if you can show me tomorrow, or the past. Where is it? I'm waiting....

There are two kinds of time in this world. Both are illusions. The first has practical value – it is time by the clock, based on simple measurements of relative motion between objects. In this case, we have the rotation of the earth on its axis and the revolution of the earth about the sun. All our units of time are based on these two measurements. Without this form of time, the world would be in perpetual chaos (unless we all chose to spend our time meditating on a mountaintop).

We are not suggesting you ignore this "physical" time – only that you stop identifying with it. Do not let physical time become your master. It is a tool for communicating in this world. It allows people to experience physical life with some semblance of order.

The other kind of time is psychological – this is your sense of time. Again, this is also an illusion. While physical time has some practical value, psychological time really has no useful purpose other than to keep you trapped in duality.

Psychological time is your sense of a "past" and "future." What does five minutes feel like? Can you imagine what you will be doing five minutes from now? What were you doing five minutes ago? The only seeming reality to this idea involves the measurement of motion. Five minutes ago on the clock, your body was probably in a slightly different position, the earth was at a different point in its rotation, etc. But other than that, does the past and future really exist at all? If so, where are they?

Psychological time is a variable (so is physical time based on Einstein's Special Theory of Relativity). Five minutes can seem like five hours if you are bored, or it can go in the blink of an eye if you are absorbed with something. However, as illustrated in the "free beer tomorrow" analogy, you cannot and never will be able to find the past or future, which ultimately means they don't exist – they are merely ideas put forth by the mind. **They are mechanisms to give the mind a sense of continuity.** But is the mind really continuous or does it just seem that way?

Is it possible to die and be reborn in every moment? Is that the secret to enlightenment? We will have more to say about that in later chapters.

Time is an Illusion

It appears that human beings are capable of seeing the past, present and future simultaneously, and that we are all potentially precognitive, meaning able to foresee the future.

Dr. Dean Radin performed an experiment where hundreds of people were hooked up to a computer and their brain impulses measured. Then images were selected at random. Two kinds of images were shown: (1) Disturbing; and (2) Calm. The vast majority of the people had their brain impulses indicate correctly which images would be shown, even before the computer had randomly generated the images. In other words, if the image was disturbing, the patient registered a disturbing impulse in their brain waves before the image was even generated, and if the image was calm, the brain waves of a calm person were registered before the image was shown.

(See the second holographic movie, Part 2, at this link: https://www.youtube.com/watch?v=vU6yCD_sEvU

The experiment is described in detail so even non-scientists can understand it.)

The scientists then go on to conclude that everything begins with the infinite field of intelligence (God), which already knows what decisions you are going to make. The "decision" is downloaded from the field into the brain, which then records it and projects it into a holographic "reality" for you to interact with and respond to with your body senses. This entire process takes, on average, about six seconds.

The conclusion is that the brain knows what decisions we are going to make before we even think about them. This would support the idea that choice is an illusion and that everything is predetermined. This also seems to indicate that it is possible to step outside the realm of time and view it from a higher place, where past, present and future are spread out before us. (Recall our example of the tree in the forest.)

*"It's like being in a movie theatre. The brain is the movie projector. And the movie you're watching [the 'external reality'] is a hologram [projected by the brain] and is not real."*

--Robert Anton Wilson

It stands to reason that if space is a holographic projection, then time as we know it would also be virtual and not real.

Lynn McTaggart, author of "The Field," states that *"We are the world. There is no 'out there' out there. There is no place where 'we' end and everything else begins."*

## The Universe Exists because Consciousness Observes It

"The observer is the observed." What does this really mean? Is it just a philosophical trick of the mind?

To investigate, let us once again consider the discussion between philosopher, J. Krishnamurti, and physicist, Dr. David Bohm, which essentially states that everything we perceive is a projection of consciousness.

In light of the Non-Locality Principle and the concept of quantum entanglement, we have already seen that the idea of separation between particles, assumed to be reality according to classical Newtonian physics, is essentially shown to be false at the quantum level.

Also, it is well known that it is not possible to have a truly independent experiment at the quantum level due to interference between the observer and the observed.

The spiritual text, *"A Course in Miracles"* states that "Ideas leave not their Source." The text essentially states that everything is an extension of the Mind of God. There is really nothing outside this Universal Mind.

Einstein stated that the more he explored the universe, the more it seemed to him to be not a giant realm, but more like a giant thought.

There is nothing outside of consciousness. There is nothing outside of the Divine. The observer is the observed.

This implies that time and space do not really exist – they are holographic images projected from a single Source. If everything "outside" of us is part of that single point, then the whole idea of "outside" is an illusion. There is no "outside" at all. Everything is contained within our one consciousness.

**The Big Bang is merely a holographic projection of this one point, which is the Mind of God.**

In Summary

Science has explored the mysteries of life, but the evidence or proof as to what is the actual reality that we are living in can only be deduced from studying both scientific and philosophical understandings. The dictionary defines "proof" as "evidence to describe a thing as true." In the realm of spiritual understanding, the evidence will be your own experience. However, as Einstein says, "*The most beautiful thing we can experience is the mysterious. It is the source of all true art and all true science.*"

The message of modern philosopher Tony Parsons also embraces recent discoveries of quantum physicists, neuroscientists and biologists.

"*To make the shift (in consciousness), you must become aware that you are not your body, mind or senses, because these can be observed. Rather, you are what is observing.*"
– Tony Parsons

This "observer" is what many mystics call the "witness" or "watcher."

"*What you actually are is a pristine awareness, or consciousness, existing here and now and expressing through your unique instrument, the individual body/mind/self that you call 'You.'*"
– Tony Parsons

You are the timeless, unchanging awareness noticing and responding to the endlessly changing drama that is called life.

# Chapter 4 - Beyond Separation – Beyond the Dream

Earlier it was observed that most human beings have an underlying sense of dissatisfaction in daily life that drives the illusory self to look for a deeper meaning. Somehow it senses that something is missing, that there must be more to so-called daily existence.

This little self finally begins to become aware that it is part of a dream world, a total-immersion, holographic "movie," and that it is playing a character in the movie.

It is like waking up from sleep. When you wake up you are in a completely different reality than where you were in the dream; the fundamental illusion is seen for what it is.

The observer is seen to be the observed – there is no separation. Both the dream character and the dream are part of the illusion. Both are projections of consciousness.

It follows that there is no separation between you and the conflict you see in the world. There is no separation between you and anything.

Everything is a mirror. There is only one Self; therefore, when you see troubles, problems, and conflicts, know that you are seeing an aspect of your concept of self being projected out into the world, which is then mirrored back in the form of "life experience."

What is consciousness? We posed this question in the last two chapters, and we will keep coming back to this question. Based on the answers of enlightened teachers and scientists, we can make the following observations:

- Everything is consciousness;

- Everything we perceive is a projection of consciousness; and

- Everything you are looking for is within you. No one can give you anything you do not already have. You already have it all but you have to dive deep inside to find it.

Once this state of consciousness is realized, there is liberation. The dream world begins to fade and awareness of the Infinite Love and Compassion of the One beyond all illusions returns to the dreamer, and he awakens from the dream.

The character in the dream dissolves, along with the dream, and the consciousness (the One who created and projected the dream and dream world) is revealed, or rather, remembered. It is at this point that you realize the true nature of your being – that the Infinite lives within you *as* you. Also happening at the same time is a lessening of the habitual identification with the ego and ego-based thoughts.

One's focus becomes riveted on the Divine Being that is our true essence. Once we begin living in and through this Divinity, the world becomes less relevant and thoughts cease to take control of our consciousness. Now there is a celebration of our joyous connection to our true reality, our own Divinity.

It is said that all forms will reach this place of ultimate Nirvana. It is also said that the substratum of all existence that we perceive in the dream play is love.

## We are Love

*"Love is a law without an opposite."*
--A Course in Miracles

*"The moment you have in your heart this extraordinary thing called love and feel the depth, the delight, the ecstasy of it, you will discover that for you the world is transformed."*
--J. Krishnamurti

This brings us to the idea that there is one field of intelligence, which we call consciousness, and so by definition, it cannot have an opposite. Therefore, the realm of duality must be illusion.

**Looking upon everything as an expression of Love, seeing even those mired in hate as unconscious expressions of Love, frees us from the world.**

*"Love created us like itself."*
--A Course in Miracles

Our true nature is Love, and therefore we share the same qualities as Love, in its pure and unconditional state. We attain a state of Love through the realization that all is God. This requires the relinquishment of all judgment and the willingness to accept what is.

*"Love is the greatest thing in life."*
--J. Krishnamurti

We are Pure Consciousness

*"The world is made of consciousness. The world is consciousness."*
--Dr. Amit Goswami

*"There is another world that is intangible, a spiritual world, that affects and influences the physical world."*
--Dr. Jeffrey Santinover

*The "higher self" or consciousness conceives reality, while the brain (illusory self) receives it, and the physical senses (dream character) perceives it. As personality constructs, you (the false self) do not actually conceive of any ideas."*

--from Daryl Anka, Bashar

In other words, the little self does not make decisions, the Higher Self does. The false self is incapable of making decisions. It can only receive decisions from the Higher Self (the I AM Presence beyond the dreamer).

Identification with the lower, or false self creates the illusion of free will, but in reality there is only God's Will (the decisions of the Higher Self).

Getting back to the original question, "What is consciousness?" you could say it is the intelligent field of energy that creates from the infinite vibrations and frequencies of the strata (the Bose-Einstein condensate). It is the Real Self that sees the false nature of the personality and the appearances of this world.

In the Bible, Jesus says at one point, *"I of myself can do nothing; it is the Father within that doeth the works."* This has been distorted to mean that we are powerless to create and that we should turn everything over to God. It is impossible to do this and remember who we are. If we are already God, how can we turn something over to our Self? We can only remember our Self, which is to wake up from the dream of duality. In truth, only our Real Self is capable of creating anything. There is no little self there to turn anything over to anyone else. The little self is merely a holographic projection, part of the dream world.

In the movie, "The Holographic Universe," there is the concept of an "Infinite I" or "I AM Self." It is claimed in that work that it is not possible to "be" this "Infinite I." Based on our definition of "Infinite I" or "Higher Self," we disagree. It is actually impossible to NOT be the Higher Self, since only the Higher Self is real.

*"<u>The only way you will ever awaken </u>is when you are totally empty of all the learnings, of all the teachings, empty of everything. Then there is freedom."*
--Robert Adams

*"God dwells in you, as you, and you don't have to 'do' anything to be God-realized or Self-realized, it is already your true and natural state. Just drop all seeking, turn your attention inward, and sacrifice your mind to the One Self radiating in the Heart of your very being. For this to be your own presently lived experience, Self-Inquiry is the one direct and immediate way."*
--Ramana Maharshi

# Chapter 5 - How to Free Yourself from the Illusion

*"No matter how many times I tell you this, you're still thinking, thinking, judging, judging, coming to conclusions, trying to work out your life. You have to let go. Totally, absolutely, completely."*
--Robert Adams

## Gaining Control over Your Mind

You will likely be in conflict with your mind when you begin the path toward Self-realization. Once you are in conflict with your mind the mind becomes stronger and stronger. It will not release you. You cannot drop the mind directly. That's like trying NOT to think of a pink elephant. You will find it is the mind trying to go beyond the mind, which, by definition, is not possible. You will eventually become depressed and decide you are hopelessly stuck in the mind.

The first step is to become aware of being unaware. Notice that you cannot even sit still for a minute or stop thinking for more than a few seconds. Wars are going through your mind.

Check yourself right now. Haven't there been thoughts running through your mind? There are always thoughts. They never seem to leave you. They are there all the time.

As long as you stay in your thoughts you will never have peace and happiness. It is that clear.

How do we deal with the 50,000 or so thoughts per day that flow through the mind? Putting these thoughts in check is a Herculean task for most. The vast majority of these thoughts are about the safety and well-being of the ego, personality and physical body.

In order to let go of these thoughts, we must stop identifying with the ego and let go of judgment.

Stop judging yourself and your individual thoughts. Simply allow them to come and go. Notice the split between "you" and "your thoughts." This split is an illusion. There is just thinking taking place, not a separate self that is doing the thinking.

In other words, the "me" in "me and my thoughts" is an illusion; it is merely another thought. Can thought really see anything at all? Isn't thought simply part of the illusion?

Do not forcibly try to stop your thoughts. That will only increase their seeming power. Even by trying to change your mind and thinking good thoughts, you are still standing in the mind. When you try and replace bad thoughts with good thoughts, you are still in conflict with the mind.

When you fall into your thoughts you might become angry. Do not identify with your thoughts. Instead, be the witness and not the subject of them. Remember the eternal Self that is living your dream character. Become aware of this present moment.

There can seem to be a great divide between the thinking mind and the ability to identify with the Presence. For a while, it seems like you go back and forth between the silence of now and the thinking mind with its incessant thoughts of the past or future. You will reach a point where you can exit the mind at will. This ability represents a turning point in your evolution. This transcendence of mind does not come about through the efforts of the ego, but rather through Divine Grace.

## Meditation

By quieting the mind, by keeping still, by not reacting, you will see truly. To the extent you can do this, you will find the mind becomes quieter and quieter. As your mind becomes quieter it begins to expand into your True Self.

True meditation involves a still mind. There is no longer any thought. But you cannot strive to attain this state. It must come of its own accord when the conditions are right for true silence.

*"Meditation is freedom from thought and a movement in the ecstasy of truth. Meditation is an explosion of intelligence."*
— J. Krishnamurti

*"To be free of all authority, of your own and that of another, is to die to everything of yesterday, so that your mind is always fresh, always young, innocent, full of vigour and passion. It is only in that state that one learns and observes. And for this, a great deal of awareness is required, actual awareness of what is going on inside yourself, without correcting it or telling it what it should or should not be, because the moment you correct it you have established another authority, a censor."*
— J. Krishnamurti, Freedom from the Known

*"The only way you will ever awaken is through silence, not through analyzing of facts. Not by sorting out good and bad, but through simple silence, letting go. Letting go of all thoughts, all the hurts, all the dogmas and concepts. Letting go of these things daily."*
--Robert Adams

The practice of meditation means to create an environment where meditation can happen. Normally, there is a sitting posture, in some practices movement, perhaps some breathing, maybe a ritual or two. These techniques cannot guarantee anything; no formality is going to ensure silence; you may have to develop your own means of inviting silence into your consciousness. All effective techniques are simply ways of assisting your mind in becoming quieter. Trying to attain inner peace is a contradiction. Trying to do anything will take you away from what you seek, because it is the ego, or false self, that is trying.

Be the witness. Your thoughts determine your perception of reality. It doesn't make a difference if they are "good" or "bad." No difference. However, so-called "bad" thoughts are generally more difficult to detach from, because they tend to draw you into the drama more deeply. Negative thoughts also trigger negative feelings. Your thoughts determine the quality of what you experience moment to moment while in the dream. A person having a lot of depressed thoughts and who identifies with and entertains those thoughts, will experience a state of depression. A person who is able to engage and qualify his thoughts in a positive way will have a happier dream state.

Thoughts are part of the illusion and take you away from your Real Self. Thoughts are part of the human experience.

Just observe yourself constantly. Become involved in the study of your thoughts – not analyzing, but watching without judgment. You are your own laboratory.

Notice the nature of your thoughts. You have "inner" and "outer" thoughts. The "outer" thoughts are the most obvious. They pertain to how to get along in the world, what to do with your earthly life, etc. How you respond to the world is up to you. But it's worth asking, "Who is responding to the so-called demands of this world?"

Your "inner" thoughts are your reactions to yourself, including self-criticism, self-judgment, self-evaluation, etc. When you have an unpleasant thought, is this thought followed by "inner" thoughts of self-condemnation? "Why do I keep thinking about this? What's wrong with me?"

Also, ask yourself, "To whom do these thoughts belong? Who's thinking these thoughts? Who gave them birth? Where do they come from? Can you tell me what your next thought will be?" You have to realize the nature of the mind first before you can transcend it.

So why do you want to go beyond the mind? If there is no mind, there's total peace and happiness. Yes!

The next step is to realize that every time you use the word "I," you are sitting inside your mind. Whenever you say the word "I," you are conjuring up images and ideas of reality that replace the actual reality.

"I" is a thought. It is not an entity. It has no reality. It is simply a thought. When you say, "I feel bad today," what entity are you talking about?

When you are saying that you feel depressed, who is depressed? The "I" is depressed. Now remember the "I" is a thought. It's not you. You must detach yourself from these ideas.

The "I" is a thought. You are not this "I." When you are able to see this, you'll be awakened. When you're able to see that you're not your story or the drama, you'll be free. You will be liberated. From now on, whenever you say the word "I," stop and think about it.

Who is the "I?" "I feel happy, I feel sick." It is the "I" that feels this way, not you. If you would catch yourself in the morning when you wake up, you'll find the True Self beyond the "I" you have fabricated from thoughts. At this point, the little "I" begins to leave you alone because you are no longer identified with it.

When you are able to transcend the "I," you will follow the Real Self back to Source. The Source corresponds to the heart center to the right side of your physical heart. You'll realize the absolute reality, which is pure awareness.

The object is to bring your focus back to Source. And you will open to total freedom and happiness.

As you learn to move beyond the ego identity (the self you thought you were), you clearly see the role the little self plays in the drama. You recognize the nature of your character and how it seems to take you away from your True Self.

The True Self is always available and is always here. There was never a time when the Self was not here. You must let go of everything by not reacting to the world. You are a Divine human being. You are not the body or the mind. You are a spiritual being. A spiritual being that has been stuck in mind.

What is the "Self" or "not Self?" What is thinking or not thinking? What is good or evil?

There is only the Self. An individual body does not really exist. In actuality, nothing exists that can be explained. Reality is beyond explanation.

Even the idea of Self or no Self has to go because it limits you. The Self that encompasses everything. All forms appear as a part of Self, and you are that.

Space and time are part of the human game. It's all on the relative plane. Earthly perception is part of the human game. When you are trapped within the relative plane or *maya*, you have a problem. But – not to worry – it's all a dream.

## Spiritual Practice

The true teacher is within you. You do not have to look for one outside. A spiritual practice, with or without a teacher, is simply a method, tool or technique that helps create the right environment for the expansion of awareness. The purpose of a spiritual practice is to help you let go of the world and enter within, the only place where true reality can possibly exist.

There are many spiritual practices. Some are designed to discipline the mind to prevent it from interfering with your peace. Others are designed to trick the mind into becoming quiet.

The greatest and most direct spiritual practice is what the Buddhists call "mindfulness." Although this term seems to imply a strong mind, what it really means is to watch, observe and notice everything that moves in your consciousness; every thought, feeling, impression, image, etc. Of course, this is very difficult for most people. Think of mindfulness as a steep, direct path to the top of the mountain – not for the faint of heart.

Shamans and mystics, like Zen masters, find ways to bypass or short-circuit the mind. Whether it is through mind-altering substances, rituals, chants, communication with spirit beings, or through koans (impossible questions), these techniques are all designed to give you a glimpse of what lies beyond the incessant thoughts of the mind.

There are thousands of spiritual practices, each having some value to some students. This book is not here to promote any particular practice, other than mindfulness. We are not Buddhists even though we are using one of their techniques as an example. This author does not subscribe to a particular creed or dogma. Every religion and metaphysical path has some value, depending on what you need and when you need it.

This book is not for everyone. Some are not ready for it. That is okay. Its purpose is simply to help you awaken.

## Enlightenment

When the mind totally disappears, this is what we call Self-realization or enlightenment. There really is no such thing as Self-realization. You are all already realized. However, there must be a breaking of the identification with the false self. You must remember who you are. You must become aware that you have been the Atman, the Avatar, all along. There has never been, nor will ever be, a time when you are separate from your Source. You have been asleep, dreaming that you are separate. The separation has never been. It is not real.

Thus, you enter a new world. The old world was simply an illusion. The old world is dead and you are alive.

This is a state that is completely different from where you have been in your imaginary world. This is a state of supreme happiness, which is your real nature – what you really are. Only it has been covered up through identification with illusion.

*"God dwells in you, as you, and you don't have to 'do' anything to be God-realized or Self-realized, it is already your true and natural state. Just drop all seeking, turn your attention inward, and sacrifice your mind to the One Self radiating in the Heart of your very being. For this to be your own presently lived experience, Self-Inquiry is the one direct and immediate way."*
--Ramana Maharshi

"<u>When divine vision is attained, all</u> *appear equal; and there remains no distinction of good and bad, or of high and low.*"
   --Sri Ramakrishna

*"Silence gives answers."*
   --Rumi

*"Why look outside?*
*Become like melting snow,*
*Wash yourself of yourself."*
   --Rumi

*"Silence is the language of God,*
*all else is poor translation."*
   — <u>Rumi</u>

# Chapter 6 - Recognizing Suffering in the Mortal Dream

Let's look at the illusion of separation from a slightly different perspective.

What is the root of suffering?

The bottom line is, as thoughts or events arise, we have a choice. The illusory character can either identify with them or recognize them to be of no real consequence, just part of the dream play. Again, the only real freedom we have within the illusion is to either accept what is occurring or to suffer the ramifications of the thoughts or events that seem to be taking place if they are of a negative nature. As one realized sage expounded, if we truly want to be Self-realized, or understand the truth of the dream, we must let go of the idea, "I am the doer." As long as you believe you are the doer, as John Lennon said, "Instant karma's gonna get you."

There is only one "doer" and that is the Infinite Self, the Source of all Creation.

Everything is going to unfold the way it's supposed to. It doesn't need any help from your imaginary self. Every step of your life has been outlined. Every move you make is determined by the Holy Self beyond your false reality. Therefore, there is no need to argue about anything. Just be still and know you are the Divine Being beyond this dream world. This predeterministic philosophy is quite liberating. If everyone's story is encrypted and predisposed to happen, who is there to blame for anything? There is no individual to be blamed. This allows for total forgiveness for what we label as the hurtful actions of another. And this also allows for total forgiveness of oneself.

All guilt and anger dissolve because there is no doer. This allows us to accept freely what appear to be other people's opinions and belief systems as well as the stances of other countries. This acceptance is total liberation from your story and the planetary movie or drama.

This does not mean you become callous and disregard the well-being of others. On the contrary, those who are liberated from the dream are often the most compassionate and do the most good in the world. Because they are no longer reacting to the dramas taking place in front of them, they are clear, calm and quiet within, and from this state of inner peace can see clearly the highest and best way to respond to what is taking place in the world.

In embracing the point of view that the ego, of itself, can do nothing, the whole vibratory frequency of the planet is raised. We might be very surprised with the results. When a human being awakens, the whole nature of the dream is seen. One can, through a limited understanding, wonder why the dream play has been written this way or that. The drama of human history has included many horrendous events and it seems a mystery as to why the story has unfolded in this manner.

Our human cognition is limited. We do not see the full spectrum. Our power lies in perceiving the events in the world with compassion, acceptance and love. This will raise the whole frequency of what is occurring in the mortal dream.

Note: There are books that go into detail on why the drama has turned out this way, such as *"Original Cause"* by Ceanne de Rohan (Four Winds Publications), or *"Soul Integration"* by Sal Rachele (Living Awareness Productions).

You must become aware that you are not the body, mind or senses. Again, you are the consciousness that is observing them. You are the timeless unchanging awareness noticing and responding to the endlessly changing drama that is life.

The drama we are currently living is an instant in eternity and is totally changeable, but not through the efforts of the ego. Predeterminism does not mean doing nothing because you don't matter. You might be tempted to say, "After all, it will turn out the way it turns out, so why bother doing anything at all?" This is a misunderstanding of God's Will vs. your little will. Your awakening is predetermined, although you might not know the day and hour of its occurrence. Your doing of good in the world might be predetermined as well, although you can continue to react with anger toward what is going on, which seems to delay your love and compassion.

If time is an illusion (as science has demonstrated), then in the end it matters not when you choose to recognize and accept the Divine Plan that is already occurring in your life, but why prolong the misery? If everything happens at once (from a higher perspective) then, as *A Course in Miracles* states, "The instant you first felt the separation (fall from grace), God's answer was already there." The course goes on to say, "All this (the dream world) has not occurred because you are as God created you." In the Bible, it states that a great sleep came over Adam, and nowhere does it imply that he had reawakened.

When you awaken you will realize the truth of that statement. It will be as though none of this (the dream) ever occurred at all, because it did not.

You are either awake or awakening, or asleep and dreaming. If you are awake, you may not be happy with the state of the dream world, but you will always be at peace. Nothing, not even a great loss, will destroy your equanimity. There is total acceptance.

If you find yourself in the quagmire of illusion, now you have the ability to gently bring yourself back to the present moment. At first it may seem hard to transcend your illusory character, but it will get easier over time.

As you flip back and forth between truth and illusions, you may find yourself observing the character traits and qualities of the persona, but you are no longer identified with that self.

When Atmananda's wife died, he had tears streaming down his face, and many people asked him, if he is a sage, why is he suffering and crying. Atmananda replied that the habit patterns of the mind respond and act in accordance with the situation but the eternal Self does not suffer.

Nisargadatta Maharaj, who embodied truth and liberation as powerfully as anyone, said he still had on occasion mental or emotional reactions or residual feelings and that when these feelings occur they become, as the years go by, increasingly fainter. With consciousness as the ocean, they are like waves and eddies that cause a passing disturbance but don't affect the overall clarity and stillness of the ocean. You notice the events and remind yourself that the problem affects only the dream character and is not who you are. You become present and remind yourself that you are not your story, but rather, you are the timeless ever-present awareness that looks at the story and experiences the emotions surrounding the story. Calmness and tranquility will return and if you are fully present with the problem, it will soon show you its own solution. As your awakening deepens and matures, you will eventually come to the place where you don't even have to remind yourself to return to Presence. Enlightenment is a no-maintenance state.

Right Action in the World

*"Before enlightenment, carry water and chop wood. After enlightenment, carry water and chop wood."*

--Zen proverb

Many people on the spiritual path are asking, "What is my dharma? How can I make a difference in the world? What can I do to end the suffering I see around me everywhere?"

If you observe those who are doing the most to help the planet, without exception they will report that "goodness" is happening through them, often without much conscious effort. Trying to do good comes from ego. Trying to do anything indicates you are still stuck in the drama.

You must allow good to be done through you. Remember, you are not the "doer." Your I AM Presence is expressing love and compassion, not your ego. The ego is incapable of love because the ego is not real. Simply get out of the way and allow your Higher Self to do the good that is needed. Allow your Real Self to direct your actions in the world. You will know when you are following your Higher Self by how you feel. Are you at peace? Are you calm and still? Or are you worrying that you are not doing enough to "save" the world?

## Accepting Suffering and Going Beyond

It has been said that pain is inevitable, but suffering is not. Another way to say this is that pain is part of the experience of life on earth, but suffering is optional. It has also been said that pain is resistance to the truth, and suffering is resistance to pain. What does this mean?

From a human perspective, pain begins during the birth process, at least physically, and then continues throughout life. Every time you stumble or bump your head, there is pain. Of course, there is also emotional pain – the pain of feeling ignored or rejected, being criticized or judged, etc. It is nearly impossible to avoid this kind of pain. The toddler often gets programmed that this is a life of pain and that moments of joy are fleeting, so we had better grab the good times while we can before they disappear.

This attitude, based on childhood programming, is partially responsible for the attachments we form later in life. When something good seems to come along, we clutch onto it and insist it remain, even if it is temporary (which it usually is).

As the Buddha said, "Attachment creates pain." And so the cycle repeats itself until we reach a state of non-attachment (enlightenment).

What about suffering? How is it different from pain? Let's look again at the idea that suffering is resistance to pain. In other words, a voice inside (the ego) might be saying, "I should not feel this pain. God must be punishing me. I must have done something wrong. I am a bad person." Now there is a classic pattern of inner conflict between "what is" and "what should (or shouldn't) be."

If there is pain, we must start by accepting it. This does not mean resigning oneself to it or staying stuck in it. There is a difference. Let's just be with the pain. Let's find out what is underneath it by going through it instead of trying to avoid it. Suffering comes from refusing to accept our pain; by refusing to look at it directly and without judgment. Ask, "What is the nature of my resistance to 'what is?' Who is resisting? What is this voice that demands that things be different from the way they are?"

Once again, the key is to enter into pure awareness – simply observing the movement of consciousness without reaction. It is the way it is. Accept it. Then, from that acceptance, right action can take place. From being fully present with "what is," we can remember our Higher Self, who knows what to do.

Let us understand Nisargadatta Maharaj's advice to become empty of all the demands we have placed on ourselves and to surrender to the pure consciousness of who we truly are.

*"You are Pure Consciousness. Your true nature is beyond description. It cannot be known with the mind, yet it exists. It is the source of everything. You become what you believe. How powerful are the effects of beliefs. Be aware of this truth. Know that you exist before knowing anything else (concepts or experiences). Have the firm conviction that you are Pure Consciousness."*
-- Nisargadatta Maharaj

"No man can seek the divine because *he does not have the capacity for such a search. But when somebody has become ready to disappear, has become ready to be a nobody, has become ready to become an emptiness, then the divine will certainly find him. Only the divine can seek for man, man can never seek the divine because even in seeking, the ego is present."*

--Osho (Bhagwan Shree Rajneesh)

*"Sacrifice is an illusion. How can there be anything to give up in order to get something better, if everything is already yours, because you are everything."*

--Sal Rachele

*"Once the true self has come into residence, you realize that you are that. It is what you are. God is the perfect expression of your own true self. There is no other and it is the same true self that exists in everyone but which is expressed through that unique and particular stained glass window of the personality, which is that common and all pervasive light, refracted through the individual expression of it."*

--Les Visible "The Dog Poet"

# Chapter 7 - The Way to find Peace in the Mortal Dream

As we enter the path of awareness we leave the world of illusion behind. We actually give up nothing. We are still standing in the same place but seeing the world through different eyes. This is the new perspective, where we leave the personal story that is assigned to us in the drama or movie of life and identify with our true nature, as consciousness. There comes with this awakening the awareness that everything is impersonal. I still can appear to plan things because planning is a habit. I am still responsible but with a deepening relaxation and welcoming of whatever is presented. Suffering is transcended because everything is seen to be "dream stuff" and there isn't even a dreamer. There is no one to be hurt, no one to be killed, no one to feel the loss of another. There is only consciousness.

Each thought that comes must be witnessed by the consciousness that exists within. Consciousness must become our true identity and the witness of all the happenings in our story. If thoughts come to us that are negative and we are living in this story, we will suffer the repercussions of the thoughts because emotions follow thoughts.

There is a formula to finding peace in the dream state. It is outlined as follows:

- Wherever you are, stop all motion;
- See the thoughts your mind is experiencing;
- See that the "I" doing the thinking is not you;
- Observe your thoughts as often as you can;
- Follow how these thoughts take you out of present time; see if you can bring yourself back to the moment;
- Once you are back in the present, you are in your natural God-state. Keep bringing yourself back every time you are tempted to identify with the ego;
- Keep repeating this process and eventually you will realize you are living in the eternal now.

Ultimately, all thoughts come from God, because God is everything. However, most thoughts arise from the part of the mind that believes it is separate. It is a paradox.

As we learn to quiet the mind, we begin to realize that all the answers are within us. We do not need to look outside for the truth. We *are* the truth.

There is nothing outside of God. Therefore, there is nothing and nobody to do battle with. We have no adversary, no enemy.

Peace comes when we realize this happy fact. If God is everything and everyone, how can there be a force outside of us constantly thwarting our every move, or looking to harm us in some way?

The mystic sees everything and everyone as God, continuously. The face of the Divine peeks out from around every tree and flower. The face of the Divine is peering out from your own eyes.

Saint Francis said, "You are looking for what is looking."

*"Do you know what you are?*
*You are a manuscript of a divine letter.*
*You are a mirror reflecting a noble face.*
*This universe is not outside of you.*
*Look inside yourself;*
*everything that you want,*
*you are already that."*
— Rumi, Hush, Don't Say Anything to God: Passionate Poems of Rumi

## Your Thoughts Prevent You from Obtaining Peace

Your thoughts cannot bring you peace because they originate within the dream world, within your illusory self. Almost every thought is a response or reaction to something in the dream play. In truth, your thoughts have no substance; they are unable to change anything of real value.

Understanding that your thoughts and everyone else's come from nowhere, we ask, "Can you tell me at this moment what your next thought will be?" If we develop the capacity to automatically qualify our thoughts, we will soon discover how false most of these thoughts are. Your thoughts are part of the illusion. Learn to go between your thoughts to the truth that dwells in the silence. How to do this? Practice being present with yourself each and every moment. At first it will be difficult because you are developing a new habit, but very soon you will not have it any other way.

## Living in the Here and Now

As indicated in the prescription outlined above on how to live a more peaceful life, it is essential to stop unnecessary thinking and to quiet your mind. It is essential to live in the here and now, forgetting the past, not worrying about the future and doing whatever is necessary in the moment to help your persona be present.

In truth, it is impossible *not* to be in the moment. The author is still waiting for someone to show her the past or future. Where are they? They seem to be in the mind that fabricated them, but do they really exist?

You will find that a lot of your thoughts are worries about the future. "What if this happens, or what if that happens?" Most of the time the things we worry about never happen, and if they do, well, that's part of the drama. Your Real Self is unaffected.

Don't be judgmental or try to change anything or anybody. Remind yourself repeatedly that you are the Atman, the Brahman, or spirit. It really helps to step back from the chatter and clamor of worldly events, most of which are unsettling and unhappy. Enter a silent state as often as you are able to. Silence is not on most people's agenda. In silence it is easier to hear and feel the truth and love that exists within us. Silence is magnificent.

*"To understand the immeasurable, the mind must be extraordinarily quiet, still."*
— J. Krishnamurti

*"Love is not of the mind, it is not in the net of thought, it cannot be sought out, cultivated, cherished; it is there when the mind is silent and the heart is empty of the things of the mind."*
--J. Krishnamurti

The Paradox of Oneness

The rishi, the saint, the sage, the mystic, have one thing in common. They are living a paradox. They are *in* the world but not *of* the world. They are One with everything, including suffering and the other elements of the drama, but at the same time, they are beyond the illusion.

Because everything is God, this dream world was, ultimately, created by God as well. Its only reality is that of vibrating energy projected outward by consciousness as thought. As the mind becomes quiet, the little self, and the thoughts it generates, become absorbed and dissolved into the God Self, and the little self ceases to exist. All thoughts become transformed in the One True Self.

You, being everywhere and everything, are omnipresent within this dream world. You are in the hearts and minds of every dreamer as he weaves his illusions. You are present in the thoughts that give rise to the imaginary self, the ego. Once the ego is quiet, the little self dissolves into the Oneness of your being.

What does it mean to be in the world but not of the world? It means you do not close your eyes to the problems that seem to surround you. You become involved with people. You engage them. You are active in the dream world (even if that means sitting on a mountaintop, which is an activity). You are not teaching how to escape from the world – as was said earlier, how can you escape from something that is not real? You are here to help others open their eyes and brush off the nightmare, while announcing the joyous news that the drama is not real.

You love your neighbor as yourself, while at the same time realizing that the little self that seems to be separate is an illusion. For a while, you are a character in the play, ready and willing to take off your mask at the appointed time. That time need not be when you shed the mortal coil. "You" can die at any moment (while in a human body).

The enlightened live in a world of enchantment because they are continuously dying to yesterday and tomorrow, and entering the eternal present. Everything is brand new, fresh, alive. There is often great joy and ecstasy.

*"When you feel a peaceful joy, that's when you are near truth."*
— Rumi

# Chapter 8 - Who am I?

You might ask, "What am I, if I am not human?" You are pure being – awareness – bliss. To realize this, is the end of all seeking and the end of all suffering. You come to this point when you begin to see that all you thought yourself to be is mere imagination. You then stand aloof as pure awareness, beyond the transient or the unreal. This is the essence of awakening.

It is not tremendously hard to attain Self-realization, but detachment is needed. It is clinging to the false self that makes the truth so difficult to see. The real is always with you. You need not wait to be what you are.

*"It takes no time at all to be what you are."*
– A Course in Miracles

Recall the author's mention of the "Who Am I?" workshop, where participants simply ask that question over and over again for several days. Words can never describe who you really are, and the purpose of this intensive process is to come to a direct realization of that. As the days go by while asking this question, the mind seems to become ever more cunning and clever in its answers, perhaps eventually arriving at the "ultimate" answer. But there is no such thing. How can there be? If words can never reach the truth the best you can hope for is that they will set you on the doorstep of truth's entrance. But if truth is everywhere, how can there be an entrance or exit? Entrances and exits are for the dream play, as Shakespeare so eloquently pointed out. Probably J. Krishnamurti's most famous quote is *"Truth is a pathless land."* In the end, all paths must go, even the inquiry, "Who am I?"

*"To reach enlightenment, all desire must go. The last desire to go is the desire to find God."*
--Osho (Bhagwan Shree Rajneesh)

Our One Being is everywhere. All paths are contained within it, and yet it is beyond all paths.

Here are a few statements that describe the author's perception regarding the nature of the Real Self:

- There is no "other."

- Basically, the experience of the essence, the Real Self, unifies everything into a singularity of One. And paradoxically, that single One is experienced from the perspective of "me" and "you." Just as everything is a projection from a singularity, everything real is still a singularity, a single point.

- For this reason, and for the sake of simplicity, I'll refer to the cosmic perspective as the God-Self

- experience. Of course, it could be labeled anything - Oneness, the One, the Only, All That Is, One-Self, etc.

- At any time, we are able to transform into and experience the God-Self. It is inevitable because that is who we are.

- Ultimately, we do not have to do anything because our awakening is predetermined in our script. One self-realized master (Robert Adams) said that awakening is already encoded within your story, so relax!

The Dalai Lama calls emptiness, "the true nature of things and events." Tony Parsons goes into a bit more detail:

*"The belief that 'I am somebody' requires all kinds of strategies in order to be a better somebody, a more successful somebody, a more happy somebody, a somebody with more pleasure, less pain and more accomplished. It's incredible how inventive we can be during this process. But maintaining this facade is the ultimate high stress undertaking because it takes a lot of work to maintain the illusion."*
--Tony Parsons

*"If the doors of perception were cleansed everything would appear to man as it is, infinite. For man has closed himself up, till he sees all things through narrow chinks of his cavern"*
--William Blake

*"Despite our instinct to polarize ourselves in the name of survival, an indescribable connection - call it love or compassion - pervades and dissolves our apparent separation. This oneness transcends physical and emotional relationships; it's a deep connection that surfaces only when the ego-laden barriers are lifted."*
--Rajeev Kurapati

*"Your True Face in the Mirror:*
*You will never have a bigger shock then the moment you realize that you have never been anything you have perceived. It is beyond mind blowing... oh, the mind is still there (when it is), but it's no longer mistaken (mis-taken) for you. You are prior to any thought or appearance. Nisargadatta said, 'You are nothing perceivable or conceivable.' However, these are just words until you see it directly, for yourself. It's an intuitive knowing that comes and goes, until finally it settles. Once this happens it becomes impossible to take yourself as anything."*
--Michael Jeffreys

## What is Self-Realization?

It is the awareness of your True Self that exists beyond the illusory self you call "me" or "I." To attain this awareness, you cannot use the mind. The mind projects thoughts, beliefs and programs about reality into the world, giving rise to a holographic image of reality that is based solely on the projection. Therefore, you must enter the stillness between thoughts in order to have a direct experience of the Oneness.

In a sense, speaking of Self-realization is a delusion. It is only because people have been under the delusion that the "not Self" is the Self and the unreal is the Real, that they have to be weaned out of it by the other delusion called Self-realization, because actually the Self is always the Self and there is no such thing as realizing it.

If you find yourself in this awareness, you give up the human belief that you will eventually die, that you will suffer intensely when life does not go your way and that you need to keep acquiring things and knowledge, even though you know nothing really belongs to you. When you realize your true Divinity, you are blessed with the understanding that you will never die. You are never separated from the "I AM" awareness. In this understanding there is no distinction between the rich and poor, the powerful and homeless; there is no distinction between nations, races, religions, or even the sexes!

Staying in this state requires silence and meditation. You experience life like a dream, because that is what it is. You welcome the good and the bad equally with appropriate response. Every day is just another moment, another show, another movie. Be amused how the day will unfold. Then close your eyes. Drown out all images. Quiet all thoughts. Bring the mind to silence. This will be your secret portal to the infinite. With your mind empty of thought there will be no stress. Soon peace will descend upon you, just stillness, with no drama. This is an introduction to the formless.

> "*The person is merely the result of a misunderstanding.*
> *In reality, there is no such thing.*
> *Feelings, thoughts and actions race before the watcher*
> *in endless succession, leaving traces in the brain*
> *and creating an illusion of continuity.*
> *A reflection of the watcher in the mind*
> *creates the sense of 'I' and the*
> *person acquires an apparently independent existence.*
> *In reality there is no person,*
> *only the watcher identifying himself*
> *with the 'I' and the 'mine.'*"
> --Nisargadatta Maharaj

"*[When the sense of a separate self dies] ...we are experiencing merely the ending of a dream or the ending of a journey in time. [When the little self dies], we are*

*immediately awakened to unconditional love. When the [illusion of a separate] body/mind is dropped there is no process of preparation or purification. There is no 'after-life' or reincarnation – these are illusions of the mind. The story is over. Not one jot could have been different. Our [illusory] existence begins and ends with this dream that has been played out. We have always been the ocean and the waves, the darkness and the light, the nothing and the everything."*
--- from Tony Parsons

Tony Parsons describes enlightenment's qualities as, "unconditional love, compassion, stillness, and joy." Enlightenment is the loss of the sense of self-hood and self-image and the eradication of the belief in a separate entity. Enlightenment also possesses another quality, which bridges the timeless and ends the illusory sense of separation. That quality is Presence, which is with us all the time but interrupted by our expectations.

*Presence is within the essence of what is. This is where aliveness resides. Presence is like what other non-dualists called consciousness. Presence is timeless and is the source of nothing and everything.*
–Tony Parsons

Now, here are some more thoughts on the true nature of reality:

- You have a body, but it autonomous. It is functioning on its own. You don't need to tell it to breathe. You don't tell your heart to beat, it just beats but it is not through your volition.

- You might say that "you" are your mind, or you have a mind that defines your existence for you. Your mind is a combination of your thoughts, beliefs, attitudes, images, etc. Your brain is part of the body. Thoughts are a collection of positive and negative responses to the dream world. Well, what about when you are not thinking. Do you cease to exist?

- You are not your thoughts.

- Surrender to the fact that there is no "you." Let it settle in. There is no you.

- Thoughts are a mental construct that in totality most people equate to the "I" that they believe they are.

- The awareness that looks out of your eyes is identical to the awareness that looks out of mine. There is only one point, the Source of everything.

- You cannot find a separate self. The thing you think of as the "I" does not exist.

- Your mind logically concludes that since thoughts, feelings and sensations exist, coming from what you think is your mind, that there is a separate you.

- Paradoxically, it does feel like there is a separate and distinct you, but what you consider as your distinct you is nothing other than the thoughts, feelings, sensations, etc., coming from the mind. Does this make a separate you?

- If you are not feelings, sensations, concepts, or what you think, then who are you?

The feeling of being you comes from consciousness – the undivided whole of awareness. It is an incredible paradox. The feeling of your existing is not coming from a separate self, even though the mind interprets it this way. That inner feeling of existing is coming from a united whole consciousness. It is not coming from a separate entity called you because there is no you. Everything that appears to be happening comes from the One that animates everything – you, me, the flowers, the trees, everything.

Ultimately, we suffer because we perceive everything as being fixed and real. The ego seems to have the ability to possess actions, people, and material things. It is only when we see through the illusion and open ourselves to truth that we become unburdened from the sorrow that seems to engulf us at times. Hence, to understand and embrace emptiness is truly the only worthwhile thing to do.

Let us state our premise once again in different words: The dreamer thinks that the dream world is real until he is awakened to the higher state where there is only one mind that projects the world of plurality. The plurality is real as long as the dream lasts. The awakened mind is Advaita (which literally means non-duality). The plurality of the dream world is perceived from the viewpoint of a dreamer who thinks he is different from the tiger and trees in the forest. The mind buries this awareness and does not allow us to experience the Divine mystery. The incredible miracle of the Oneness of all things is hidden within the drama of the dream world.

*"So long as anyone thinks that there are two ultimate realities, he is mistaken. When he has come to know that there is but one, he is right. This is what is being proved to us every day, on the physical plane, on the mental plane, and also on the spiritual plane."*
--Albert Einstein

As one expands in consciousness and becomes aware of higher and higher dimensions of existence, it is as if these dimensions fold up and disappear behind him. From the mountaintop, there is only One Reality beyond all dimensions and levels. Swami Vivekananda sums it up nicely:

*"So it is with regard to the soul; the very question of birth and death in regard to it is utter nonsense. Who goes and who comes? Where are you not? Where is the heaven that you are not in already? Omnipresent is the Self of man. Where is it to go? Where is it not to go? It is everywhere. So all this childish dream and puerile illusion of birth and death, of heavens and higher heavens and lower worlds, all vanish immediately for the perfect. For the nearly perfect it vanishes after showing them the several scenes up to Brahmaloka [the ultimate levels of reality]. It [the illusion] continues for the ignorant."*

*"Time, space and causation are like the glass through which the Absolute is seen. In the Absolute there is neither time, space nor causation."*

*"...this separation between man and man, between nation and nation, between earth and moon, between moon and sun. Out of this idea of separation between atom and atom comes all misery. But the Vedanta says that this separation does not exist, it is not real."*
--Swami Vivekananda

*"When Presence is opened up we enter into oneness, which is what we really are. This is the bridge between the dualistic world and enlightenment. Once crossed it is no more. This is the open secret. In Presence there is awareness, which is the light that enters the darkness. When light enters darkness it dissipates those illusions that interrupt oneness. Awareness brings the light to evaporate all that is illusory."* --Tony Parsons

*"Life is...a dream, until you wake up but...who is it that wakes up? What are you upon awakening? Are you what and who you were when you were dreaming, and even when you think you have awakened, might you not still be asleep? We've all had those dreams where we thought we woke up, only to find out we were still dreaming."*
   --Les Visible (the "Dog Poet")

# Chapter 9 - How do You Know You're Free?

When you finally realize that you truly are the One Self, it makes no difference what you are thinking. Good thoughts, bad thoughts, or any kind of thoughts are irrelevant. All thoughts are clouds that cover up the sun. Thoughts cannot see; they can only interpret reality. Beyond them, you have a deep sense of peace.

When realization happens you will know the truth of who and what you are, beyond all the beliefs and stories that previously gave you identity. No matter what is happening you will always feel a deep sense of peace. There will be an abiding tranquility in the core of your being; your fundamental peace and well-being are ever present despite what seems to be taking place in the world around you. And this will be true whether you are waking, sleeping or dreaming. You may still see suffering happening in the world but you will always be at peace. Your love and compassion will radiate out from the center of your being into the midst of the pain and misery. Nothing, not even a great loss, will destroy your sense of balance and poise.

It's difficult to deny the truth of something once you've had your own experience of it. Truth is both subjective and objective.

The truth exists within and beyond time. It is in the past,

present and future, which do not actually exist. It is in the eternal now, the only time there is.

*"People like us, who believe in physics, know that the distinction between past, present and future is only a stubbornly persistent illusion."*
  --Einstein

*"The intuitive mind is a sacred gift and the rational mind is a faithful servant. We have created a society that honors the servant and has forgotten the gift."*
  --Einstein

## Ending the Separation

The enlightened state is both ordinary and profound. You see directly "what is," with no reaction by thought. There is nowhere to go and nothing to do, and yet you are going and doing wherever and whatever your True Self directs. This is what is meant when we discussed right action. There is a natural order and beauty to the universe. Everything is unfolding according to the perfect Divine Plan, whether or not your little self believes or likes this.

When you look at a tree, flower, or person, there is simply the direct experience of that, without the mind interpreting, evaluating, judging, comparing and worrying.

You look beyond the illusions and see the truth of that wondrous thing you are beholding.

You might become aware of levels of beauty and wonder that you never noticed before. Everything might shimmer and shine. An all-pervading love and ecstatic energy might take hold of you. Even if human feelings arise, such as anger, fear or sadness, there is a deep peace underneath these feelings. They come and go quickly because they are of no actual substance.

Time seems to stand still. The past has dissolved. It is as if it never existed in the first place. Past, present and future blend into one single Creation, and this Creation extends forever in all directions. You have reached a state of desirelessness. You realize you have everything. You realize you are everything. In this timeless moment, you are reborn, again and again, each time new, fresh, unknown and unknowable.

It matters not whether you get caught in the illusion again, because you know that your Real Self is forever beyond illusion. You cannot really get caught in the illusion because there is nothing to get caught in and there is no self to get caught. Perhaps you laugh at your silly little human self, then reach out and tenderly embrace it and give it the love it needs to wake up.

The ability to laugh at yourself is critical. Most people take themselves way too seriously. If you feel sad about the suffering in the world, then just feel sad. Accept it. Celebrate it. Do something about it if you feel moved. But just allow it to be what it is and remember who you really are.

*"All people on the planet are children, except for a very few. No one is grown up except those free of desire."*

— Rumi

"You are already the Self. Therefore *realization is common to everyone. Realization knows no difference in the aspirants. This very doubt, 'Can I realize?' or the feeling, 'I have not realized' are the obstacles. Be free from these also."*

--Ramana Maharshi

"God has spun this eventful cosmic *play on the stage of time to entertain us, but we take the shadows as serious realities! There is only one Serious Reality - and that is God."*

--Paramahansa Yogananda

# The Last Chapter – Only Consciousness Exists

*"The only freedom is the freedom from the known."*
— J. Krishnamurti

Almost everyone believes in some sort of life after death. Whether it is being reborn in a different body, or going to some pre-appointed location such as heaven or hell, death is almost never regarded as the final chapter. It is the persona, the ego, that fears death because it is attached to its illusion of being. Underneath its insistence on maintaining itself is the dreaded realization that it is but a tiny ripple on the surface of the sea. It is afraid of being swallowed up by the vastness of the ocean. It is afraid of losing its "specialness," its uniqueness.

Some psychologists believe that all the anxiety the human persona experiences has, at its bottom line, the fear of death. We maintain that the fear of death comes from the belief in separation from the whole. Feeling cut off from Source, we try to prolong our little life, even with its misery and suffering, in order to maintain the illusion of control we desperately seek.

The fear of death comes from attachment to the known, and death represents the unknown. To die to the known is to be reborn in every moment. This can only happen when the self is emptied of all content, all images, ideas and concepts. It is not necessary to drop the body in order to die to the past and enter the eternal present. Every moment is brand new, as if you are seeing the world for the first time. This is what "*A Course in Miracles*" calls the "real world" or "true perception." But ultimately, this is still an illusion, for truth lies beyond all perception.

Although it might seem as though one will be caught in the mortal dream forever, there is an appointed time for awakening; for one to reach Self-realization. That destiny is in the hands of your True Self. The ego has no control over when you will awaken. Even if you put tremendous effort into awakening, it is still in God's hands. When the time is right, you will awaken. All souls will eventually perceive the nothingness in all forms and then gently come out of the dream.

However, in the dream state, very few have activated the ability to see this transformation. At the point that the persona dissolves into what the world considers death, the human mind no longer produces thoughts or forms. The mind as an objective reality disappears.

The many teachers quoted here have said that everything in the movie or drama is a projection or a manifestation of the mind. With no mind there is no universe. There is no remembrance of the dream, the movie or the play. Without the mind, without the persona, we enter a land of enchantment. This is the real heaven. In this magical place there is no duality. There is nothing to worry about. There are no thoughts of the past or future. Nothing exists except complete Oneness. This can evoke feelings anywhere from deep, joyful peace and acceptance, all the way to ecstasy. At this point the individual self is completely dissolved and merged totally with the One. Everything originally perceived as form dissolves into the One. This is an egoless state. There is nothing but pure, unconditional love, and in the reality of this nothingness, everything becomes apparent and real.

If this is not your vision, you are still attached to the false imagination, the belief in time. The liberated imagination is a whole different thing. True creativity springs forth from liberation. You could say it is an automated process, but the joy of creating is anything but predictable. Spontaneous delights await you as you put away the fears of yesterday and tomorrow and move into the eternal present.

The persona fades into its original state of infinite being. Neither ego nor mind really exists but only seems to. In this absolute state they are dissolved, or rather, awareness sees that they never were in the first place.

Everyone will eventually reach this place of ultimate Nirvana. Everyone will at some point realize this state of supreme love. Some realize it while still in physical form.

## More on the State of Enlightenment

When you are perceiving a state of duality, it seems as though you have been trapped in this duality for a long time, perhaps with a distant memory of having been in some heavenly place. However, when you awaken from the dream of duality, it is as though the state of duality never existed. You realize you have been in this non-dual state all along, and the dream seems like a mere flicker of the eye, barely interrupting the eternal now.

## The States of Satori and Samadhi

Although it is impossible to "lose" the state of enlightenment, it is certainly possible to cover over the experience with the business of life on earth. In other words, it is possible to get drawn back into the drama after having awakened, just as you may experience another night of dreaming tonight after waking from last night's dream. This going in and out of enlightenment is an illusion, but it can seem very real. When enlightenment seems to be temporary, it is called a "Satori" experience.

At some point, one is able to remain in a state of enlightenment without losing awareness periodically. Such a continuous state of enlightenment is called "Samadhi."

Comedian Bill Hicks sums up the interplay between truth and illusion quite well:

*"We are all one consciousness experiencing itself subjectively. There is no such thing as death; life is only a dream, and we are the imagination of ourselves."*
– Bill Hicks

*"The world is like a ride in an amusement park, and when you choose to go on it you think it's real because that's how powerful our minds are. The ride goes up and down, around and around, it has thrills and chills, and it's very brightly colored, it's very loud, and it's fun for a while. Many people have been on the ride a long time, and they begin to wonder, 'Hey, is this real, or is this just a ride?' And other people have remembered, and they come back to us and say, 'Hey, don't worry; don't be afraid, ever, because this is just a ride."*
– Bill Hicks

*"Enjoy the ride."*
--Francis Lucille

*"Happy is the man who is nothing."*
— J. Krishnamurti

## Conclusion

There are only so many words that can be used to describe what is and will forever be beyond words. After all, the word is not the thing described – it cannot be, by definition. The word "tree" is not the same as the actual living entity called by that name.

Always remember that we are only pointing to the truth. We can never successfully experience the truth through words. This book is meant to be a catalyst, to trigger a level of awakening within you. No book, teacher or path can open the door to enlightenment, but such methods can bring you to the doorstep and gently set you down in front of it. Your Holy Divine Self is the one that opens the door and helps you walk through it. Your task is to simply be ready to enter into a state of emptiness. Only an empty vessel can be filled (with truth).

The author encourages you to explore the writings and teachings of the many masters who are quoted herein. Put each one to the test. Never blindly believe anything that is said in this book or any other. Investigate. Explore. Observe.

As with any book or source of information, it's important to only embrace what resonates with you. Throughout this book, if something doesn't resonate with you, it is not your truth. If it does resonate with you, embody (live) the truth of it. Then, once you've embodied its truth, you can discard the book. This is the purpose served by all books and teachings.

*"The truth shall set you free."*
--Jesus

# Bibliography

**A Course In Miracles** (1978)
Foundation for Inner Peace, Tiburon, CA.

**Adyashanti,** Emptiness Dancing (2006)
Sounds True Press, Boulder, CO

**Alexander, Thea**, 2150 AD (1976)
Macro Books, Tempe, AZ

**Allen, James,** As a Man Thinketh (1938)
DeVorss & Co., Marina Del Rey, CA.

**Anka, Darryl,** Bashar, Blueprint for Change
New Solutions Publishing, Simi Valley, CA.

**Bauman, Bill, Ph. D.** Oz Power: How to Click Your Heels and Take Total Charge of Your Life (2005)
Center for Soulful Living, St. George, UT

**Ceanne de Rohan,** Right Use of Will (Vol. I), Original Cause (Vol. II & III) (1986)
Four Winds Publications, Santa Fe, NM.

**Dreaver, Jim,** End Your Story, Begin Your Life (2011)
Amazon Books

**Haunt, Eryk,** The Rumi Card Book (2000)
Journey Press, Boston, MA

**Hurtak, J.J.,** The Keys of Enoch
Academy of Future Science, Los Gatos, CA.

**Keyes, Ken, Jr.**, The Hundredth Monkey (1980)
Vision Books, Coos Bay, OR.

**Krishnamurti, J.,** Nature of the Mind (2007)
Krishnamurti Foundation, Ojai, CA

**Krishnamurti, J., and Bohm, David, Ph.D.,** The Ending of Time
(Dialogue, 1985)
Harper & Row, New York, NY

**Krishnamurti, J.,** Krishnamurti's Notebook (1974)
Harper & Row, New York, NY.

**Krishnamurti, J.,** Flight of the Eagle (1972)
Harper & Row, New York, NY.

**Krishnamurti, J.,** Think on These Things (1970)
Harper Collins, New York, NY

**Krishnamurti, J.,** Commentaries on Living: First Series (1956), Second
Series (1958)
Quest Books, New York, NY

**Leonard, Jim & Laut, Phil,** Rebirthing: The Science of Enjoying All of
Your Life (1980)
Trinity Publications, Hollywood, CA.

**Maharaj, Sri Nisargadatta,** I Am That (1973)
Translated by Maurice Frydman
Acorn Press, Durham, NC

**Maharaja, Sri Srimad Bhaktivedanta Narayan Gosvami,**
Journey of the Soul (2010)
Spectrum Printers, India

**Maharshi, Bhagavan Shri Robert Adams,** The Silence of the Heart,
Jan.-June 1991, July-Dec. 1991, 1992 (three volumes)
No-Self Press, Santa Monica, CA

# Bibliography

**Maharshi, Ramana,** Talks with Sri Ramana Maharshi (1994)
Translated by Sri Ramanasramam Tiruvannamalai
T.N. Venkataraman, Madras, India

**Mooji,** Vaster than Sky, Greater then Space (2016)
Sounds True Publishing, Boulder, CO

**Osho (Bhagwan Shree Rajneesh),**
The Path of the Mystic (2007)
Osho Media International, New York

**Osho (Bhagwan Shree Rajneesh)**
The Art of Dying (1999)
Osho Media International, New York

**Parsons, Tony,** As It Is (The Open Secret of Spiritual Awakening) (2000, 2$^{nd}$ Edition 2002)
Inner Directions Publishing, Carlsbad, CA

**Parsons, Tony,** Invitation to Awaken (Embracing Our Natural State of Presence) (2004)
Inner Directions Publishing, Carlsbad, CA

**Rachele, Sal,** Life on the Cutting Edge: (1$^{st}$ ed. 1994, 2nd ed. 2016)
Living Awareness Productions, Wentworth, NH

**Rachele, Sal,** The Real History of Earth (2015)
Living Awareness Productions, Wentworth, NH

**Ramakrishna, Sri,** The Original Gospel of Sri Ramakrishna
Sri Ramakrishna Math Internet Store

**Ramakrishna, Sri,** First Meetings with Sri Ramakrishna
Translated by Swami Prabhananda
Sri Ramakrishna Math Internet Store

**Rumi, Jalal al-Din,** The Essential Rumi
Translated by Coleman Barks & John Moyne
Coleman Barks / HarperCollins, San Francisco, CA

**Rumi, Jalal al-Din,** The Book of Love
Translated by Coleman Barks & John Moyne
Coleman Barks / HarperCollins, San Francisco, CA

**Salwak, Dale,** The Wonders of Solitude (1995)
New World Library, Novato, CA

**Silva, Jose,** The Silva Method
Silva Method International, Inc., Laredo, TX.

**Skarin, Annalee,** Ye Are Gods
DeVorss & Co., Marina Del Rey, CA.

**Spalding, Baird J.,** The Life and Teachings of the Masters of the Far East (Five Volumes) (1962)
DeVorss & Co., Marina Del Rey, CA.

**Talbot, Michael,** The Holographic Universe (1991)
Harper Perennial, New York NY

**Tolle, Eckhart,** A New Earth: Awakening to Your Life's Purpose (2005)
Dutton Press, Vancouver, BC

**Tolle, Eckhart,** Stillness Speaks (2003)
Namaste Publishing, Vancouver, BC

**Tolle, Eckhart,** The Power of Now: A Guide to Spiritual Enlightenment (1999).
New World Library, Vancouver, BC

**Vatsyayana.** The Complete Kama Sutra (1994).
Translated by Alain Danielou
Park Street Press, Rochester, VT

# Bibliography

**Yogananda, Paramahansa,** Man's Eternal Quest: Collected Talks and Essays on Realizing God in Daily Life, Volume I (2000)
Self-Realization Fellowship, Los Angeles, CA,

**Yogananda, Paramahansa,** Autobiography of a Yogi (1946, 2nd Ed 1995)
Self-Realization Fellowship, Los Angeles, CA,
The Philosophical Library, New York, NY.

*We are the actors in the confinement of the separated personality and behind this is the illuminated self that is everything all at once and which is asleep within the dream state of the individualized personalities that come and go... on and on like waves upon the sea. The waves are a temporary permutation of the sea. Identification as a wave is a reflection of the mind in its mortality and identification with the sea is a reflection of the immortal mind in its enduring permanence.*

--Les Visible (the "Dog Poet")

# Index

Paradox —
who is the doer

rendering enlightenment

① perfect Divine order
② enlightenment in
here & now —

seems life